FLOORS AND STAIRWAYS

TIME
LIFE ®
BOOKS

Other Publications:

THE ENCYCLOPEDIA OF COLLECTIBLES
WORLD WAR II
THE GREAT CITIES
THE WORLD'S WILD PLACES
THE TIME-LIFE LIBRARY OF BOATING
HUMAN BEHAVIOR
THE ART OF SEWING
THE OLD WEST
THE EMERGENCE OF MAN
THE AMERICAN WILDERNESS
THE TIME-LIFE ENCYCLOPEDIA OF GARDENING
LIFE LIBRARY OF PHOTOGRAPHY
THIS FABULOUS CENTURY
FOODS OF THE WORLD
TIME-LIFE LIBRARY OF AMERICA
TIME-LIFE LIBRARY OF ART
GREAT AGES OF MAN
LIFE SCIENCE LIBRARY
THE LIFE HISTORY OF THE UNITED STATES
TIME READING PROGRAM
LIFE NATURE LIBRARY
LIFE WORLD LIBRARY
FAMILY LIBRARY:
   HOW THINGS WORK IN YOUR HOME
   THE TIME-LIFE BOOK OF THE FAMILY CAR
   THE TIME-LIFE FAMILY LEGAL GUIDE
   THE TIME-LIFE BOOK OF FAMILY FINANCE

HOME REPAIR
AND IMPROVEMENT

FLOORS AND STAIRWAYS

BY THE EDITORS OF
TIME-LIFE BOOKS

TIME-LIFE BOOKS
ALEXANDRIA, VIRGINIA

HOME REPAIR AND IMPROVEMENT

Editorial Staff for Floors and Stairways

Editor: William Frankel
Assistant Editor: Stuart Gannes
Designer: Anne Masters
Picture Editor: Adrian G. Allen
Associate Designer: Kenneth E. Hancock
Text Editors: William H. Forbis, Jim Hicks, Brian McGinn,
Ellen Phillips, Mark M. Steele
Staff Writers: Thierry Bright-Sagnier, Stephen Brown,
Steven J. Forbis, Lee Greene, Lydia Preston,
Brooke C. Stoddard, David Thiemann
Art Associates: George Bell, Michelle Clay, Mary Louise Mooney,
Dale Pollekoff, Lorraine Rivard, Richard Whiting
Editorial Assistant: Eleanor G. Kask

Editorial Production
Production Editor: Douglas B. Graham
Operations Manager: Gennaro C. Esposito
Assistant Production Editor: Feliciano Madrid
Quality Control: Robert L. Young (director), James J. Cox (assistant),
Michael G. Wight (associate)
Art Coordinator: Anne B. Landry
Copy Staff: Susan B. Galloway (chief), Lynn D. Green,
Florence Keith, Celia Beattie
Picture Department: Dolores A. Littles, Rose-Mary Hall-Cason

Correspondents: Elisabeth Kraemer (Bonn); Margot
Hapgood, Dorothy Bacon (London); Susan Jonas,
Lucy T. Voulgaris (New York); Maria Vincenza Aloisi,
Josephine du Brusle (Paris); Ann Natanson (Rome).
Valuable assistance was also provided by
Carolyn T. Chubet, Miriam Hsia (New York).

THE CONSULTANTS: Bill McPherson has worked in the carpet industry, in both manufacture and installation, since 1929, and is now the superintendent of a Washington, D.C., carpet-installation firm. He has contributed to instruction manuals on carpet installation and developed refinements of installation tools.

Victor M. Casamento is an independent builder who designs and constructs custom homes in the suburbs of Washington, D.C.

Harris Mitchell, special consultant for Canada, has worked in the field of home repair and improvement for more than two decades. He is editor of the magazine Canadian Homes and author of a syndicated newspaper column, "You Wanted to Know," as well as a number of books on home improvement.

Roswell W. Ard is a consulting structural engineer and a professional home inspector in Northern Michigan. He has written professional papers on wood-frame construction techniques.

R. Daniel Nicholson Jr. is an assistant production manager and estimator for a Washington, D.C., home remodeling service.

Contents

COLOR PORTFOLIO: Floors and Stairs as Art   64

1 Restoring Damaged Floors   7
Quick Cures for a Wood Floor's Ailments   8
Supports That Bolster a Sagging Floor   14
Putting a New Face on an Old Wood Floor   24
The Care and Repair of Resilient Floors   28
Some Easy Repairs for Hard-surfaced Floors   32

2 New Floors: A Wealth of Choices   37
Getting a Room Ready for a New Wood Floor   38
Installing a Wood Floor Board by Board   40
Eye-catching Patterns in Sheet and Tile   46
Embedding Stone and Ceramic Tiles in Mortar   52
Pouring a Concrete Floor for a Basement   56
Resurfacing a Concrete Floor   62

3 The Craftsmanship of Stairways   65
Intricate Structures, Simple Repairs   66
Retreading a Stairway   72
Opening a Floor for a New Stairway   76
Two Spacesavers—Disappearing and Spiral Stairs   80
Building Simple Basement Stairways Step by Step   84
A Craftsman's Pride: The Prefab Stair and Railing   88

4 Carpets for Warmth and Softness   97
Estimating and Installing Wall-to-wall Carpet   98
Cushion-back for Easy Installation   110
The Right Way to Carpet a Stairway   112
Unseen Repairs for Unsightly Stains and Tears   116
Keeping Carpets Spotless   123
Two Ways to Launder a Carpet by Machine   124

Credits and Acknowledgments   126

Index/Glossary   127

Restoring Damaged Floors

Contemporary floor and staircase construction is a synthesis of time-proven designs with modern materials and installation techniques. Prefinished and prefabricated materials make it surprisingly easy to improve on a house by installing or restoring floors of gleaming wood or tile, sturdy concrete or soft carpet. Rented professional tools can help with the big jobs, such as pouring a new concrete slab, laying carpet or building a staircase; synthetic adhesives, floor finishes and concrete additives make the repair of tile and concrete, once a task for professionals, an everyday affair.

Perhaps the most basic flooring material is plywood, a combination of wood and synthetic glue. Flexible, strong and virtually unwarpable, it provides a firm base for any floor from basement to attic. Laid over concrete *(pages 38-39)*, it helps protect finish flooring from moisture; glued to joists, it is a stronger subfloor than traditional wood strips. It is a good base for marble, slate or ceramic tile, and, combined with a pad of insulating material, makes an economical soundproof floor.

For a new staircase you can use both prefabricated materials and rented tools. You can order a prefabricated traditional staircase, a spacesaving spiral stair or a disappearing staircase that can be installed in a few hours. For some installations you will need professional tools, such as a precision miter box for shaping the curves of a balustrade *(pages 90-95)*. This can be rented, along with a variety of tools used for flooring. A power nailer, for example, simplifies the job of installing prefinished flooring. The nailer butts the strips tightly together and drives the nails home in a single operation *(page 43)*. When you pour concrete, a power troweler will eliminate painful hours of work on hands and knees *(page 63)*. Knee-kickers and power stretchers are tools for pulling carpets smooth and tight *(page 106)*; electric jackhammers and telescoping jack posts enable you to make large structural repairs once left to professionals.

Any flooring from attic to basement needs regular maintenance and occasional repair. Floors are intimately linked to the structure of a house and natural shifts in the structure put stress on them. Other enemies of floors are moisture, abuse and age. Whatever the cause of the damage, repairs usually are possible. Some are major projects—replacing the supports beneath a sagging floor, for example *(pages 14-23)*—but most require only the right materials and a few professional tricks. You can replace or tighten worn or loose flooring *(pages 8-13)* or sand yellowed or stained wood, then refinish the floor with permanently transparent polyurethane *(pages 24-27)*. Similarly, new adhesives ease the repair of resilient flooring *(pages 28-31)*, and new bonding agents simplify the resurfacing of concrete floors.

Quick Cures for a Wood Floor's Ailments

Although wood, the most common flooring material, is one of the most durable, it does crack, stain, burn and loosen, causing it to squeak or bounce. Fortunately the remedies are simple.

Cracks can be filled, stains and burns sanded away and loose boards retightened in a number of ways. In the event of serious damage, you can replace boards without leaving any surgical scars. Most squeaks arise from subflooring that is no longer firmly attached to the joist below. When the ceiling underneath the floor is unfinished, have someone walk on the floor while you stand below searching for movement in the subfloor over a joist. The squeak can then be eliminated by filling the gap with wedges (opposite, top). If the subfloor is inaccessible, refasten the subfloor to the joist by driving nails through the finish floor above.

Squeaks can also result from rubbing between loose finish floorboards. Ask someone to walk over the noisy area while you watch for play in the floor and feel for vibrations. Where the subfloor is accessible, the squeaky boards can be secured from below (opposite, bottom). Where it is not, first try remedies that do not mar the finished surface. Force powdered graphite, talcum powder, wood glue or triangular glazier's points into the joints between boards. Should these solutions fail, nail through from above; be sure to drill pilot holes first, since hardwood flooring is difficult to nail.

Squeaks and vibrations may also indicate that the bridging is poorly installed, rotted or inadequate. It should provide reinforcement for all joist spans of 8 feet or more. If it does not, install prefabricated steel bridging, which comes in sizes to fit between joists spaced at 12, 16 and 24 inches. Install solid blocking in place of bridging wherever the joists are unevenly spaced. Cut the blocks to fit tightly between the joists, using 2-inch lumber of the same thickness as the joists. Line them up with the bridging and drive 16-penny nails through the joists into the ends of the blocks, or in cramped quarters, drive eightpenny nails through the blocks into the joists.

Even more common than squeaks are cracks arising from humidity and temperature changes, which cause boards to shrink unevenly. Cracks can be plugged with a mixture of sawdust and penetrating sealer. Use sawdust from the floor itself, gathering the dust by sanding boards in a corner of a closet. Work four parts sawdust and one part sealer into a thick paste and trowel it into the crack.

Surface defects, such as stains and burns, can be erased by sanding if they do not go too deep. To determine the extent of the damage, go over the blemished area with a wood scraper. If the defect starts to lift out, the board can be saved by refinishing. Otherwise, the damaged boards must be pried out of the floor and replaced (page 11). When replacing rotted floorboards be sure to inspect for decay in the surrounding subfloor. With an ice pick or awl, pry up some wood. If it feels spongy or cracks across the grain, rot has set in. Treat lightly decayed subfloors with a preservative containing pentachlorophenol, but if the rot has penetrated through the wood the board must be replaced.

Anatomy of a wood floor. A typical wood floor is constructed in layers. Parallel 2-by-8-inch joists, laid on girders and braced by diagonal bridging, provide structural support for the subfloor. In older homes the subfloor is often made of wide planks or tongue-and-groove boards, which are sometimes laid diagonally for extra stability. Today sheets of ¾-inch plywood are preferred, and they are usually glued as well as nailed to the joists. A moistureproof and sound-deadening underlayment of heavy felt or building paper is laid atop the subfloor.

The final layer is the finished flooring, most commonly strips of oak, ¾ inch thick and 2¼ inches wide, that have tongues and grooves on sides and ends so they interlock when installed. They are attached by driving and setting eightpenny nails at an angle above the tongues, where they will be concealed by the upper lips of the adjoining grooves (inset).

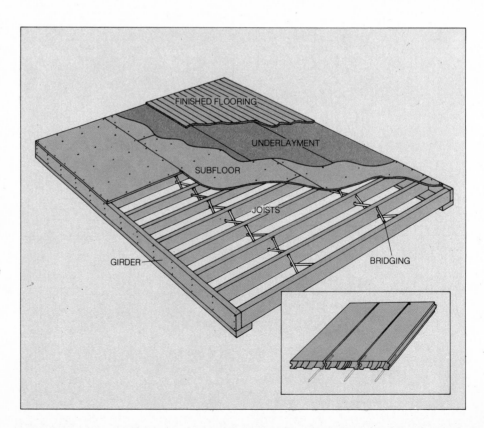

Eliminating Squeaks

Shimming the subfloor from below. Wedge a wood shingle between the joist and a loose subfloor to prevent movement. Do not force the subfloor boards upward or you may cause boards in the finish floor to separate.

Securing inaccessible subfloors. Through pilot holes drilled in the finish floor, drive pairs of eightpenny finishing nails into the subfloor and joist below. Angle the nails toward each other. Set the nails and cover them with wood putty.

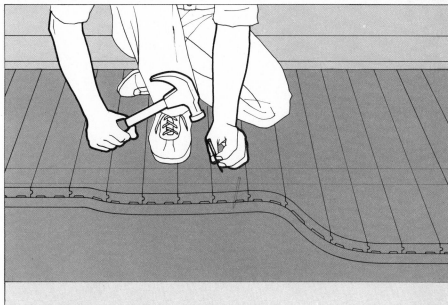

Anchoring finish floorboards from below. Insert screws fitted with large washers into pilot holes drilled through the subfloor and drive them into the finish floor. Use screws that will reach to no more than ¼ inch below the surface of the finish floor. To make the holes in the subfloor, use a drill bit with a diameter at least as large as that of the screw shanks, so that the screws will turn freely in the subfloor. Avoid penetrating the finish floor by marking the thickness of the subfloor on the bit with a ring of tape.

Next drill pilot holes into the finish floor with a bit slightly narrower than the screws. As you turn the screws, their threads will bite into the finish floorboards and pull them tight to the subfloor.

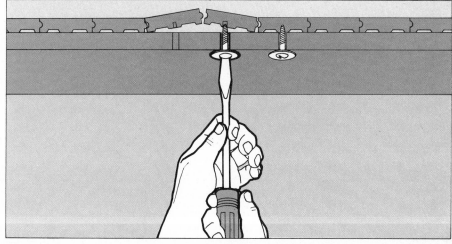

Silencing finish flooring from above. To stop finish floorboards from rubbing together, force glazier's points—the triangular metal pieces that secure glass into frames—into the joints between the boards. Coat the points with powdered graphite and set them below the surface with a putty knife. If the pressure of the knife is insufficient to push the points down, use a hammer and small piece of scrap metal to tap them into place. Insert one point every 6 inches until the squeak is eliminated.

GLAZIER'S POINTS

Installing steel bridging. Hammer the straight-pronged end of the bridging into one joist near the top. Then pound the L-shaped claw end into the adjacent joist near the bottom. Alternate the crisscross bridging pattern from joist to joist.

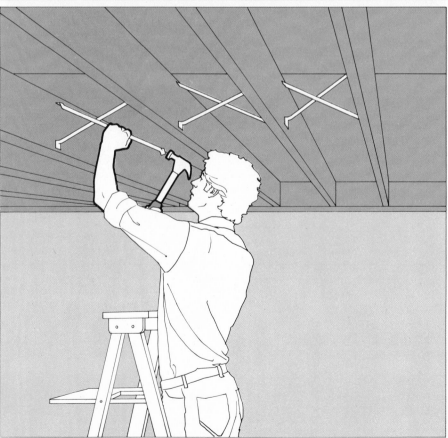

Custom-made Patches for Injured Boards

Replacing damaged boards is a job to put off until winter, when dry furnace heat will shrink the wood and make the gaps between pieces larger, permitting maximum play for sliding in replacement boards. Old floors, having acquired wider gaps over the years, are often easier to work on than new ones.

Cut out damaged boards in a staggered pattern with end joints no closer than 6 inches. Then take a sample to a lumberyard to get matching replacements. To install the new ones, follow the sequence illustrated; you will be able to wiggle most of the boards into position, sliding them forward or sideways and blind-nailing them so the repair is invisible. If a board proves obstinate, or is too wide for the space to be filled, plane it on the groove side until it fits. Only one or two should have to be dropped into place from above and face-nailed.

1 **Starting to remove a board.** Make vertical cuts across damaged boards with a 1-inch wood chisel, keeping its bevel side toward the portion of the board to be removed. Then, working back toward the vertical cut, angle the blade and drive the chisel at about 30° *(inset)*, along the board. Repeat this sequence until you have cut all the way through the board.

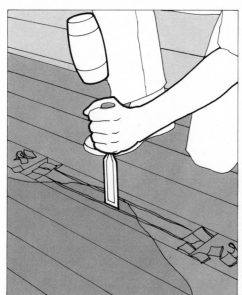

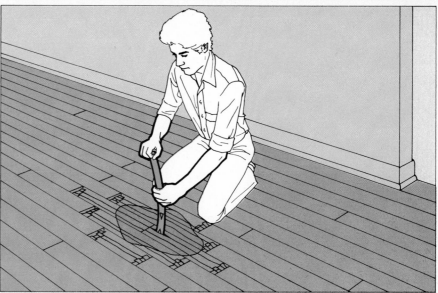

2 **Splitting the board.** Make two rows of incisions with a chisel along the face of a floorboard that has been channeled *(above)*. Pry the board up just enough to split the wood. Proceed until the boards to be removed are split *(right)*.

3 **Prying the board out.** Insert a pry bar into a lengthwise crack in a damaged board. Pry the middle strip out, then the groove side and finally the tongue side. Work from the center of the damaged area, and be careful not to damage good boards. Remove or drive down—with a nail set—exposed nails.

4 **Inserting a new board sideways.** Using a scrap piece of flooring—one that has a clear groove in its end to fit over the tongue of the replacement piece—as a hammering block, wedge a cut-to-size replacement into place, grooved side over the tongue of the preceding course.

5 **Blind-nailing a board.** Drive and set eightpenny finishing nails at a 45° angle through the corner of the tongue of the replacement. Pilot holes are not essential but may be helpful. If existing boards around the repair have separated slightly, try to match their spacing by inserting thin shims such as metal washers between the new board and the old one while driving the nails.

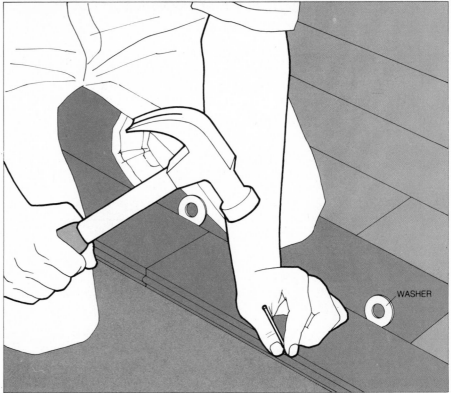

WASHER

6 Inserting a new board lengthwise. To slide a replacement between two boards, lay it flat on the subfloor and work the tips of its tongue and groove into those of the existing pieces. Using a scrap hammering block, tap it all the way in.

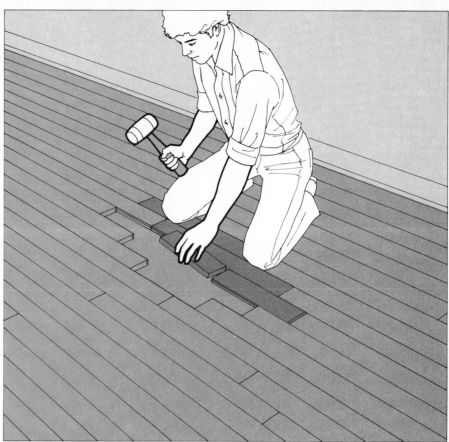

7 Inserting a new board from above. With the last few pieces, which cannot be slid into place, chisel off the lower lips of their grooves as indicated by the dashed line above. Then gently tap the board into place from above.

8 Face-nailing. To fasten the last replacement boards, which offer no access for blind-nailing, you must drive eightpenny finishing nails every 12 inches into predrilled pilot holes. Drill the holes about ½ inch from the edges of the face. Then set all face nails and cover them with putty that has been tinted to match the color of the boards.

Supports That Bolster a Sagging Floor

A dip in a floor is irritating, but not necessarily dangerous. If you have such a dip, measure it by the method shown on the opposite page. A small dip, less than ¾ inch deep and 30 inches long, can be repaired in the same way as a squeak, with hardwood wedges driven between a joist and the subfloor *(page 9)*. A larger sag is a symptom of real trouble. If it occurs in conjunction with some such seemingly unrelated problem as a sticky door, cracked plaster or leaky plumbing, it may eventually be followed by structural damage in the supporting framework of girders, posts and joists. The solution is to raise the floor and reinforce or replace the faulty supports.

Sags usually occur in older houses, built with wood posts and girders rather than steel columns and beams. They are most common on the first floor, which is generally accessible from underneath if you have to make repairs. If you have a second-story sag, an entire floor or ceiling may have to be torn out to get at the trouble, but the repair techniques are the same as those used downstairs.

The repair for a sag depends on its cause, and your first task is diagnosis. Inspect the framework underneath the floor for faulty construction *(below)*. Test for rot and insect damage by stabbing an awl into joists, girders and posts. If you find rotten wood—that is, wood that feels spongy and does not splinter—paint it heavily with penetrating preservative. A honeycomb of small holes is a sign of termites; call an exterminator at once.

To straighten a floor before making permanent repairs, jack up the joists or girder under the sag. Always use a screw jack, which is stronger and more reliable than the hydraulic type, and grease the threads before you begin. If you are working in a basement, rent a house jack—essentially a telescoping metal post fitted with plates at the base and top *(opposite, center)*. If there is only crawl space, use a contractor's jack—a squat, bell-shaped jack with a screw that extends about a foot *(opposite, bottom)*.

Once a sagging joist has been jacked up, it can be permanently straightened by doubling—that is, by nailing a new joist to the weak one *(page 16)*. The technique works even on a badly rotted joist, so long as the ends that rest on the girder and foundation wall are sound and the wood in between will hold nails. A joist that has rotted through must be replaced *(page 17)*. Before starting either job make sure that pipes, electrical wires and ventilating ducts will not prevent you from slipping the new joists into place. You will have to move any obstruction or have a professional do it; in some cases it may be easier to leave a jack in place as a permanent support and not try to repair or replace failed joists.

Jacking is also the first defense against a sag in a girder, but the final remedy is more complex. If a girder sags over a post, a jack on either side of the post will raise it. But the jacks must be left in place and set on concrete footings; it is often easier to replace the post with a steel column *(pages 18-19)*. Similarly, a sag in the middle of a girder can be jacked up, but jacking is not always best. The girder must be in good condition and made of pine, fir or some other softwood; oak beams are too stiff to be straightened. A better solution is to replace the wood girder with a steel beam *(pages 20-23)*.

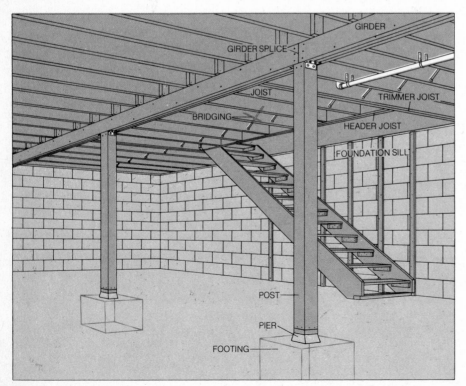

Why floors sag. This drawing shows the horizontal and vertical supports that carry the weight of the ground floor *(page 8)* in a typical house. Beneath the subfloor are joists, laid in parallel rows, outer ends resting on the foundation sills. Bridging *(page 10)* strengthens the joists and keeps them in alignment. In the center of the basement the joists rest on a wood girder. The ends of the girder rest in pockets in the foundation wall; the center is supported by wood posts on concrete piers, anchored in footings.

Shifts in the positions of these parts can cause sags in the floor above. Any of the wood members could be damaged by rot or termites. Posts that are not set on piers will absorb moisture from the basement floor, and posts that have piers but no footings are likely to sink. The built-up girder shown, made of overlapping lengths of lumber, would sag if it were spliced in the middle of a span rather than over a post. The header and trimmer joists that frame the stairwell carry extra weight and must be doubled *(page 79)* to keep them from sagging. Finally, joists that have notches or holes for electrical and plumbing lines should be reinforced. For that reason it is best when installing such lines to leave the joists intact if possible, as shown.

Jacking Up a Floor

Measuring a sag. Lay an 8-foot straightedge—a 2-by-4, an iron pipe or best of all, a rigid strip sawed from the uncut edge of a sheet of plywood—across the sagging area, measure the gap between the straightedge and the floor and mark the floor where the sag is deepest.

Measure from the mark on the floor to two different reference points—walls or stairways, for example—that lie at right angles to each other and that also appear in the basement. In the basement, take measurements from the reference points to position the jack.

Jacking from a basement. If you are straightening a floor—and do not plan to reinforce it—lock the tubes of a telescoping house jack with its steel pins, set the bottom plate on a 4-by-8 pad, and while a helper steadies a 4-by-6 beam at least 4 feet long between the joists and the top plate, screw the jack until the beam presses against the joists. Use a level to be sure the jack is plumb then nail its plates to pad and beam.

Once a day raise the jack 1/16 inch—about a half turn—until the floor is level. If necessary, slip an 18-inch pipe over the jack handle for leverage. Caution: a faster rate of jacking can cause structural damage.

If you plan to double or replace joists, remove their bridging and, when you set up the jack, insert 2-by-6 blocks on the beam between joists. Jack the floor 1/4 inch higher than level.

Jacking from a crawl space. Set a contractor's jack between a pad and a beam, following the instructions above for using a telescoping house jack. Turn the screw of the jack until the beam presses against the joists. In most crawl spaces, the jack will not rise from the floor to the joists even when fully extended. To raise the base of a jack, set its pad on a pyramidal framework called cribbing, made of rough hardwood 6-by-6s, available from dealers in structural timber. Stack the beams in parallel pairs, with each pair at right angles to the one beneath it; the top beams should be about 18 inches apart.

Raise the jack 1/16 inch a day—one-eighth turn on most contractor's jacks—until the sag disappears.

STEEL PINS

PAD

JACK HANDLE

Help for Weakened Joists

If you plan to double or replace a joist, be sure you remember to remove the bridging, if there is any, from both sides of the sagging joists before jacking them *(page 10)* and insert 2-by-6 blocks between the temporary beam and the joists. Replacing the bridging with the blocks provides the room you will need to slip new joists into place. After the repair is completed, lower the jack slowly—no more than $1/16$ inch a day—so the new joists gradually adjust to their load. Then put in new prefabricated steel bridging or—in odd-sized joist spaces created by doubled joists—solid wood blocking.

A doubling joist should match the height and thickness of the old joist, but it should be short enough to fit between the girder and foundation sill; a replacement joist should match the old one in every dimension. All joists should be straight, structural-grade lumber without cracks or large knots; if rot or termites have been a problem, use lumber that has been pressure treated with preservatives. Before you install the replacement, sight the edges to the crown, a slight rise in the center of one edge. Set this edge against the subfloor—the joist will be forced straight by the weight it bears.

Doubling is a straightforward operation: the new joist is nailed to the old

one. Replacing a joist is more complex. You support the floor during this job by placing an extra new joist beside the old one; only then can you cut out the old joists and install a new one in its place. And since there is not enough room between girder and subfloor to turn a new joist into position, you must shave strips from the bottom edge, set the joist in place, then force it up against the subfloor with shims *(opposite, top left)*.

Two specialized tools speed a tedious part of joist repair: removing the nails that fasten old joists and bridging. In the narrow space between joists you can expose embedded nailheads with a wood chisel and pull the nails with a claw hammer, but it is simpler to use a nail claw, a 10-inch steel bar with a sharp, curved claw at one end. Drive the claw beneath the nailhead with a hammer and then pull on the bar, which acts as a lever to withdraw the nail. The protruding points of the nails that once secured the floor to the joist must be cut off before a new joist can be installed—they cannot be driven up into the subfloor without damaging the finish floor. It is possible but awkward to cut them flush with the bottom of the subfloor with a hacksaw; a more efficient tool is a pliers-like cutter called a carpenter's nippers.

Doubling a Joist

Attaching the new joist. After removing bridging and jacking the floor ¼ inch above level *(page 15)*, have a helper hold a new joist tight against both the old one and the subfloor; then fasten the old and new joists together with 16-penny nails, staggered top and bottom every 12 inches. Clinch the nails—that is, hammer the protruding points flat—and install new bridging or solid blocking *(page 10)*.

To double a notched joist, cut two strips of 2-inch board 6 feet long and narrow enough to fit between the subfloor and the notches. Set the boards above the notches, one board on either side of the joist, and nail all three together from both sides with twenty-penny nails.

Replacing a Joist

1 Shimming the joist. Plane the joist ends to make notches 18 inches long and ¼ inch deep (*inset*). Remove the nails and the blocks holding the old joist to the girder and the foundation sill; then set the new joist 1½ inches from the old one, the notched edges resting on the girder and the sill, so that the joist from the other side of the girder is sandwiched between the two. Force the new joist tight up against the subfloor by driving ¼-inch hardwood shims in the notches.

2 Removing the old joist. Cut through the weak joist at points near the girder and the foundation sill with a saber saw. Use a pry bar to pull the joist away from the nails that hold it to the subfloor and cut the protruding nail ends flush with the bottom of the subfloor.

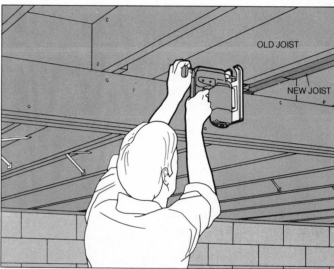

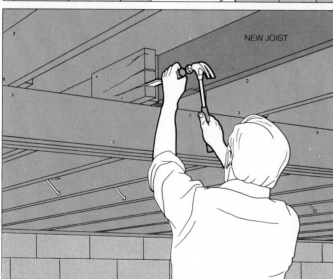

3 Splitting out the joist ends. With a wood chisel, split the ends of the old joist that remain on the girder and foundation sill. Remove the pieces with a pry bar and remove protruding nails. Then install and shim a second new joist in the old one's place (*see Step 1*).

4 Nailing the joists in. Nail the new joists to the one they sandwich at the girder, using 16-penny nails on both sides; then nail 2-by-4 wood spacers at 3-foot intervals between the new joists, using 16-penny nails. Toenail the joists to the girder and sill. Nail in new bridging or blocks (*page 10*) in line with existing bridging and nail in blocks above the girder and sill. Complete the job by driving eightpenny finishing nails down through the finish floor into the joist.

A Stand-in for a Failing Post

When a girder sags at the top of a wood post, the trouble is in the post, not the girder. Either the post's footing (if it has one) has sunk or the post itself has been attacked by rot or termites. Both problems have the same solution: replace the post with a steel column supported by a new footing. You will need a building permit, and some of the work involved is strenuous—remove the old wood post, break through the basement slab with a rented electric jackhammer, dig a hole and pour a new footing.

The key to a strong post is its footing. The size and depth of footing you need depend on the load it must bear, on soil conditions and, in unheated basements or crawl spaces, on the depth of the frost line—that is, the point of deepest penetration of frost below the ground. A footing 2 feet square and 22 inches deep is typical, but you should check your building code for the dimensions required in your locality. If your house is built on fill or if the span between the posts that support the girder is more than 12 feet, consult an architect or civil engineer. A typical footing requires less than a cubic yard of concrete, an amount that can easily be mixed by hand *(page 34)*. If you need more, rent a mixer or have concrete delivered in a ready-mix truck *(page 60)*.

Adjustable steel columns, available at lumberyards and building-materials dealers, are made of 11-gauge, 3-inch pipe fitted with screws like those on telescoping jack posts. Get a column 4 inches longer than the distance between the basement slab and the bottom of the girder, so the screw can be anchored in concrete when you patch the slab *(Step 5)*.

1 **Removing the old post.** To clear the way for the new column, jack up the girder and pull the old post out. Set up telescoping jacks 3 feet to either side of the post, nailing their top plates to the girder. Lift the girder ⅟₁₆ of an inch a day until it is level and the post no longer supports any weight. Remove the nails or lag bolts that fasten the post to the girder. With a helper, tilt the top of the post clear of the gird-er and lift the post up and off the vertical steel dowel that connects it to the concrete.

If the girder is spliced over the old post, reinforce the splice before jacking the girder. Using a hacksaw, cut away the post cap or straps that secure the splice and nail 3-foot pieces of ½-inch plywood across the splice, using 30 eightpenny nails on each piece.

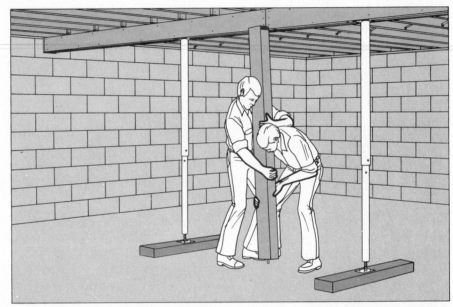

2 **Digging the footing.** On the basement floor, mark off a footing of the size required by your building code and, wearing goggles and gloves, break through the concrete slab along the marks with a rented electric jackhammer. Beginning inside the footing marks and working outward, break out easy-to-handle chunks of concrete with a series of cuts. Hold the jackhammer perpendicular to the slab at the start of each cut; then when you have chiseled out a groove, tilt the handles slightly toward yourself and lean firmly.

When you have broken up the slab and any other concrete within the footing marks, dig a hole of the depth required by the code. Clean out all loose dirt, spray the hole with a hose and pour the footing while the hole is wet *(Step 3)*.

3 Pouring the footing. Fill the hole with concrete to a point 4 inches below the floor. Drive a shovel into the wet concrete several times to eliminate air bubbles, then level the surface with a straight scrap of lumber. The concrete must cure for two weeks: cover it with polyethylene sheeting and keep the surface wet by sprinkling it with water twice a day (*page 61*).

4 Bolting the column. Set the steel column on the footing and turn the adjusting screw until the top plate of the column rests against the girder. Center the plate at the marks left by the old post and, using the holes in the plate as a guide, drill pilot holes into the girder for ⅜-inch lag bolts. Bolt the plate loosely to the girder so you can still move the column slightly at its base.

5 Making the column fast. Move the bottom of the column by tapping it with a hammer until the column is perfectly plumb, checking from all sides with a level. Tighten the adjusting screw until the column begins to bear the girder's weight, then tighten the bolts that fasten the column to the girder. Lower the temporary jacks ¹⁄₁₆ inch a day until they can be removed.

To finish the floor around the column, mix a wheelbarrow of concrete, coat the footing and the edges of the slab with a bonding agent (*page 34, Step 3*), and fill the hole so that it matches the surrounding floor (*page 61, Step 5*).

Replacing a Tired Girder

A wood girder that sags in one place is not too serious a problem; it can be jacked straight and supported with a new steel post (*pages 18-19*). Several sags, however, are a sign of fundamental weakness in the girder. Since girders are the largest structural members in a house and must support not only the first floor but all the floors above it and part of the roof, multiple sags are serious indeed. The best remedy is to replace a weakened wood girder with a steel one.

If the girder is in a low crawl space, you will need professional help; normally this repair involves cutting a hole in the foundation wall and sliding a single 20- or 30-foot beam through it and into position. In a basement you can obtain a building permit and then do the work yourself by installing the steel girder in several sections, spliced together over supporting posts. Measure the girder you are replacing. You need the same total length of

beam spliced over the same number of posts; add 5 inches to each of the end sections to allow for the parts of the girder that rest within girder pockets in the foundation wall.

From a steel dealer order S8 × 18.4 beams (I beams that are 8 inches thick and weigh 18.4 pounds per foot), plus adjustable steel columns to replace the old posts, bearing plates for the girder pockets and splice plates to strengthen the joints between girder sections. The dealer will cut the sections to the lengths you specify and drill holes for the splice plates and the posts beneath them.

Replacing a girder differs from other structural floor repairs. Instead of jacking the floor level at the start of the job, you must support it, sag and all, with a framework of a 4-by-4 shoring on both sides of the girder (*Steps 1-4*). Then remove the old girder, install a new one and jack the new girder until the sag is gone.

1 Building the shoring. Lay the parts of the shoring—top plates, bottom plates and vertical posts—on the basement floor and toenail the posts to the top plate before you raise the shoring into place. Use straight 4-by-4s, laid end to end across the floor, to form a top plate as long as the girder. Lay several shorter 4-by-4s next to them to serve as bottom plates. Using a pencil and a combination square, mark lines 3½ inches apart across both plates to indicate the positions of the vertical posts; mark the first pair of lines 2 feet from the wall, and repeat the marks every 4 feet along the length of the plates.

Measure from the bottom of the joists to the basement floor at the lowest point of the sag (*page 15*), then cut 4-by-4 posts 7 inches shorter than this distance to allow for the thickness of the plates. Toenail the posts to the top plate at the marks you have made, using double-headed eightpenny nails, two to a side. Build a second shoring framework in the same way to support the joists on the other side of the girder.

BOTTOM PLATES

TOP PLATE

POSTS

2 **Nailing the shoring in place.** Set the bottom plates on the basement floor, parallel to the girder and 3 feet to either side of it and have two helpers raise the first section of top plate and posts; the top plate should touch the lowest joists and the posts should rest on the marks on the bottom plate. Toenail the posts to the bottom plate with eightpenny double-headed nails.

3 **Shimming the framework tight.** Insert wedge-shaped shim shingles under each joist (*inset*) from both sides of the top plate. Make sure the posts are perfectly plumb—if necessary, tap them into position with a hammer—then hammer the wedges tightly in. Add sections of shoring in the same way until you have erected a framework from wall to wall on each side of the girder.

JOIST

SHIMS

TOP PLATE

POST

4 **Fastening the joints.** Toenail top-plate sections together with eightpenny double-headed nails and add an extra post under each joint, toenailing it to both sections of the top plate. Tighten shims that have worked loose.

With the shoring firmly in position on both sides of the old girder, you can remove the girder by a method similar to the one for removing a joist (*page 17, Steps 2 and 3*). First, pull out the toenails that fasten the joists to the girder. Then saw the girder into pieces, cutting it 1 foot from each foundation wall and from each post. To prevent pieces of girder from falling on you, have helpers support each piece as you complete the saw cuts. Pull the end pieces out of the girder pockets and remove the posts (*page 18*).

5 **Chiseling out girder pockets.** Mark off an outline on the foundation wall for the enlargement of each existing girder pocket and, wearing goggles and gloves, enlarge the pocket to accept the new girder with hammer and cold chisel. Each pocket should be 6¼ inches wide to accommodate a bearing plate (*below*), and 5 to 7 inches deep. To determine its height, measure from the bottom of the joists to the basement slab at the lowest point of the sag; the bottom of the pocket should be 9 inches lower than the sag.

If the foundation wall is made of hollow masonry blocks, tamp the cores beneath the girder pockets solidly with mortar.

6 **Installing bearing plates.** Lay a ½-inch bed of premixed mortar on the bottom of each girder pocket and, using a hammer, tap a steel bearing plate 6 inches square and ¼ inch thick into it; when the plate is well embedded, check with the spirit level in the head of a combination square to make sure it is perfectly horizontal. Let the mortar cure for seven days; keep it wet by sprinkling the area with water daily.

BEARING PLATE

MORTAR BED

7 **Lifting the girder into place.** With the aid of helpers—one for each 3 feet of girder length—lift one end of an end section into the girder pocket and set it on the bearing plate; rest the other end temporarily on a sturdy stepladder.

8 **Supporting the girder.** Make temporary U-shaped braces of three 2-by-4s fastened with two 16-penny nails at each corner (*inset*). While your helpers hold the section of girder tight against the joists, centered between the marks left by the old girder, set braces snugly around it every 32 inches. Then secure them with two 16-penny nails driven through each vertical 2-by-4 into the joists.

Install another braced section of girder in the pocket in the opposite wall. Lift each of the center sections onto two stepladders, then have your helpers raise these sections against the joists while you nail braces around them.

9 **Jacking the new girder.** Set up telescoping jacks (*page 15*) 3 feet from the end of each girder section, placing 2-inch oak blocks between the steel beam and the top plates of the jacks. Before jacking the entire girder, check the joints between sections; if the ends do not line up so that the splice plates can be bolted on (*Step 10*), jack the lower end of each pair 1/16 inch a day until all are in bolting alignment. Then raise all the jacks 1/16 inch a day until the girder is straight and the sag disappears. The ends of the girder that rest in the pockets will be lifted by the jacking; place steel shims 6 inches square on the bearing plates to support the girder when the jacks are removed. The girder will gradually lift the joists from the temporary shoring and the shoring will loosen. When it no longer supports the joists, take it down.

OAK BLOCK

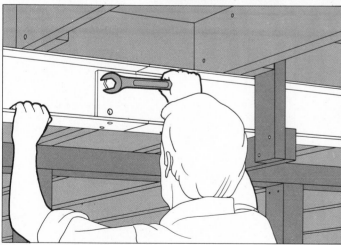

10 **Bolting the girder together.** Bolt the sections of girder together with splice plates—rectangular plates of 1/4-inch steel with predrilled holes near each corner. If two sections are misaligned, tap them into position with a light sledgehammer.

11 **Fastening the girder to the joists.** Fit beam clips—rectangular plates of sheet metal with V-shaped notches cut into one side—over the top flange of the girder and nail one to every other joist on both sides of the girder. If beam clips are not available, drive 16-penny nails into the bottom of each joist on both sides of the girder and bend them over the flange. Install steel columns (*pages 18-19*) and remove the temporary wood braces. Lower the jacks 1/16 inch a day until they can be taken out.

Putting a New Face on an Old Wood Floor

Your varnished wood floors are so worn and scuffed that no amount of waxing and polishing will restore their gloss. Or perhaps you have decided to expose the natural texture and grain of a painted floor. In either case, you must refinish your floors. It is a four-stage job: sanding off the old finish, bleaching out stains, treating the wood with a sealer that gives the floor the tone or coloring of your choice and applying a new, durable, polyurethane-based finish.

A refinishing job calls for professional equipment, available from most tool-rental agencies. You will need a drum sander, in which sandpaper is fitted over a large revolving cylinder; make sure the machine you rent has a tilt-up lever that lifts the spinning drum from the floor (not all have this feature). Also rent an edging machine with a rotating disk for hard-to-get-at areas that the drum sander cannot reach. You will also need a respirator to block the dust raised by sanding, and ear muffs to deaden the sound of the sander—a brutally noisy machine. Finally, to smooth the floor after each coat of sealer or new finish, rent a professional polishing machine; it polishes with a round pad of steel wool.

To help determine the cost of these rentals, estimate the time the job will take—normally, you can sand and seal 200 to 250 square feet of flooring in a day. You can economize by completing the work with the drum sander and edger before you rent the polisher, and use two workers simultaneously, if possible—one to operate the drum sander while the other operates the edger.

You need to use sandpaper of three grades—coarse, medium and fine. The coarse paper for the first sanding may have any of a variety of grit ratings, depending on the existing surface of the floor. To remove paint or to sand rough floorboards, start with a very coarse, 20-grit paper (the lower the grit rating, the coarser the paper). To take varnish or shellac off a strip or plank floor, use a 36-grit paper; for parquet or herringbone floors, use a 50-grit paper. For the second sanding, use a medium, 80-grit paper, and for the final sanding, fine, 100-grit paper.

Have the dealer supply you with plenty of sandpaper—at least 10 sheets and 10 disks of each grade for an average room. You will pay only for the paper you actually use. Be prepared during the job for sudden, accidental wastage; a protruding nailhead can tear a sheet of sandpaper to shreds in a split second. Before leaving the shop, check that the machines are working, that their dust bags are clean and that you get any special wrenches you may need to load the drum sander (have the dealer show you the loading method). Because sanders need grounding, they must have three-pronged plugs; if your house has two-slot receptacles, you will need grounding adapters.

To prepare a room for sanding, remove all the furniture. If you prefer not to take the drapes down, fold them over a coat hanger hung on the drapery rod; then slip a large plastic bag over them and seal it with tape. Remove the floor registers and cover the vents with plastic. Tighten any loose boards and replace boards that are badly cracked or splintered (pages 11-13). Using a nail set, drive protruding nailheads one eighth of an inch below the surface of the floor, and to make sanding the edges of the floor easier, remove the shoe moldings from the baseboards (below). Sanding produces highly flammable dust: turn off all pilot lights and electrical appliances. Seal the doorways leading into the work area with plastic and open the windows for ventilation.

Sanding Down to the Bare Boards

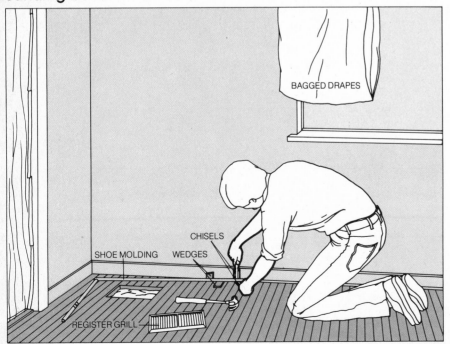

BAGGED DRAPES

CHISELS

SHOE MOLDING   WEDGES

REGISTER GRILL

1 Removing shoe molding. Beginning at a doorway, and using two sharp chisels a few inches apart, gently pry the molding away from the baseboard and up from the floor. You may have to tap the chisels lightly with a hammer to insert them. When you have loosened about 1 foot of the molding, slip small wood wedges behind and under it to prevent it from snapping back into place. Advance along the length of a section of molding, repeatedly prying out the molding and moving the wedges. As you remove each section, number it so you will know where to replace it after the job. When all the sections have been removed, pull out any finishing nails that remain in the floor or baseboard.

2 **Loading the drum sander.** With the sander un-plugged, thread a sheet of sandpaper into the loading slot, turn the drum one full revolution and slip the other end of the sheet into the slot; then tighten the paper by turning the nuts at both ends of the drum with the wrenches provided by the dealer. (On the widely used model shown here, the paper is tightened when you turn the left-hand wrench away from you and the right-hand wrench toward you.) When using fine paper, insert a folded paper wedge of the same grade between the two ends to keep them from slipping out of the slot *(inset)*.

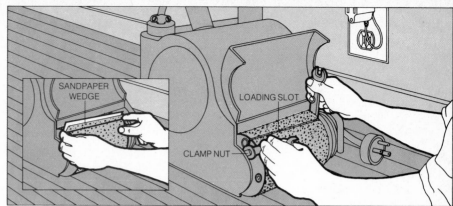

SANDPAPER WEDGE

LOADING SLOT

CLAMP NUT

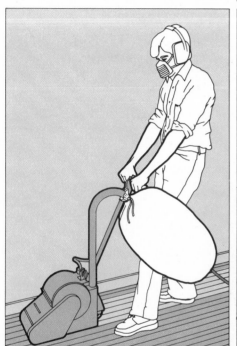

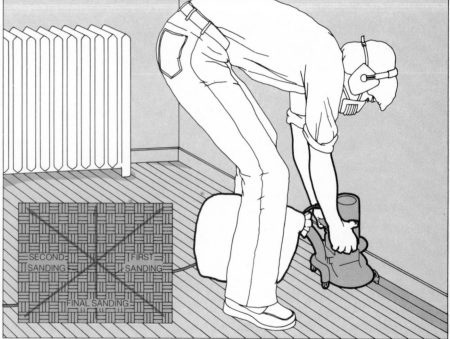

SECOND SANDING

FIRST SANDING

FINAL SANDING

3 **The first sanding.** Lift the drum from the floor with the tilt-up lever, start the sander, and when the motor reaches full speed lower the drum to the floor and let the sander pull you forward at a slow, steady pace. Sand a strip or plank floor along the grain of the wood; on parquet or herringbone patterns, which have grains running two ways, do the first sanding in a diagonal direction. When you reach the far wall, raise the drum from the floor, move the cord behind you to one side, then lower the drum and pull the sander backward over the area you have just sanded. Caution: keep the sander in constant motion to prevent it from denting or rippling the wood.

Then lift the drum and move the machine to the left or right to overlap the first pass by 2 or 3 inches. Continue forward and backward passes, turning off the sander occasionally to empty the dust bag. When you have sanded the whole width of the room, turn the machine around and sand the strip of floor against the wall.

4 **Second and third sandings.** Load the edger with coarse paper and sand the areas missed by the drum sander. Now repeat both the drum and edge sandings, first with medium paper, then with fine. On strip or plank floors, the second and third drum sandings, like the first, should be made with the grain. On parquet or herringbone floors *(inset)*, do the second sanding on the opposite diagonal to the first, and the final sand-ing along the length of the room.

5 **Scraping the tight spots.** In areas that neither the drum nor the edging sander can reach, use a paint scraper to remove the finish. At a radiator, remove collars from around the pipes for a thorough job. Always pull the scraper toward you, applying a firm, downward pressure on the tool with both hands, and scrape with the grain wherever possible. Sharpen the scraper blade frequently with a file. To complete this stage of the job, sand the scraped areas by hand.

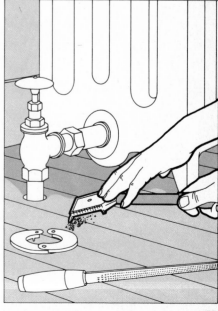

Two Protective Coats That Seal and Beautify

A new floor finish will last a long time—and so will any blemishes that are visible beneath it. Before you seal a floor, check it for stains that were not removed by sanding. If you cannot remove them by hand-sanding, use undiluted household bleach. Wearing gloves and goggles, apply a small amount of bleach to the center of the stain. Wait a few minutes to see how much the bleach lightens the spot, and then apply enough to blend the stained area with the rest of the floor. When you get the right tone, wash the bleached area with warm water and let it dry. Then vacuum the floor and go over it with a tack cloth, a rag moistened with turpentine and varnish, to pick up all dust before applying the sealer.

To fill the pores and emphasize the grain of the wood, use an oil-based penetrating sealer. Such sealers come in both natural wood hues and a clear, colorless form, and unlike conventional wood stains, they sink deep below the surface and cannot be scuffed or walked off.

Some, known as pickling stains, are tinted with pigments that give a floor an arbitrary color—blue or green, for instance—but accentuate the grain so that the floor retains the look of wood.

When a penetrating sealer has sunk into the wood, any excess remaining on the surface must be wiped off promptly before it dries. One person can apply the sealer and mop it up, but two workers make the job faster and easier (top right). For a pickling stain, two workers are essential to prevent discolorations from the uneven drying of excess sealer.

For a final protective glaze over the sealer, select a finish made with polyurethane, a synthetic resin that becomes exceptionally tough as it cures or hardens. Older finishes—varnish, shellac, lacquer and wax—yellow with age, wear easily and must be completely removed when a floor needs refinishing; a polyurethane finish is non-yellowing and far more durable. And, if it is never waxed, it can be renewed simply by running a polisher loaded with steel wool over the floor and adding another coat of finish.

1 **Applying penetrating sealer.** Wearing rubber gloves, lay on the sealer with a rag in long, sweeping strokes along the grain of the wood while a co-worker wipes up the excess. Start next to a wall and away from the door (so that you will not have to walk over wet sealer to get out of the room) and apply the liquid liberally over a strip of floor 3 feet wide. Between eight and 20 minutes after it is applied, the sealer will have penetrated the wood, leaving shallow puddles of excess liquid on the surface. At this point your helper, using rags in both hands, should begin mopping up. Start applying a second strip of sealer as your co-worker begins, and try to work at a pace that keeps both of you moving together with your knees on dry floor until the job is almost finished. On the last strip, the helper must do his part while backing across wet sealer to the door. Let the sealer dry for about eight hours.

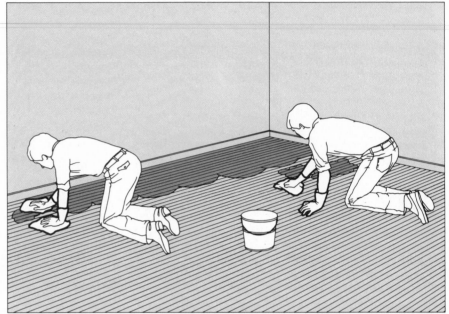

2 **Filling cracks and holes.** When the sealer has dried, force wood putty into cracks and nail holes with a putty knife. To match the color of the sealed floor, mix your own putty with dust from the final sanding and enough sealer to make a thick paste. Scrape off excess putty. When the surface of the putty has dried, hand-sand the filled areas with 100-grit paper.

3 **Smoothing the sealed wood.** Run a polishing machine loaded with fine steel wool over the floor to cut down irregularities in the surface caused by tiny bubbles in the sealer coating. To load the polisher, use a precut pad of steel wool obtained from the rental agent; fit the polisher with a heavy-duty scrub brush and press the pad into its bristles (*inset*). Scour the edges and corners of the floor by hand with small pads of steel wool, then vacuum the entire floor and go over it thoroughly with a tack cloth.

STEEL WOOL PAD

SCRUB BRUSH

4 **Finishing the floor.** Apply polyurethane finish to the main part of the floor with a long-handled mohair roller, and to edges and corners with a small brush; if you are working alone, do the edges and corners first. When using the roller, work along the grain and apply the finish slowly and evenly. Wait at least eight hours, then smooth the surface with fine steel wool (*Step 3, above*). When you have gone over the floor with a vacuum and tack cloth, apply a second coat of finish across the grain. Wait another 24 hours for the floor to dry before replacing the shoe moldings, floor registers and radiator-pipe collars.

The Care and Repair of Resilient Floors

Resilience is the ability to bounce back, and most types of resilient tile or sheet flooring—cork, asphalt, linoleum, rubber, vinyl and vinyl-asbestos—do that in several senses. They are more or less bouncy underfoot. But also their tough surfaces bounce back from wear and stains *(page 46)* to retain their like-new appearance for many years. Common-sense precautions help. A resilient floor should be kept as dry as possible, even when being cleaned *(page 31),* so that water does not get underneath it and destroy the bond of the adhesive that holds it in place. Resting furniture feet on plastic or rubber coasters will help protect the floor from punctures and gouges. When furniture or appliances too heavy to lift must be moved across a resilient floor, slide them over pieces of hardboard.

If, in spite of careful maintenance, your resilient floor is accidentally damaged, you usually can repair the injuries yourself—or at least reduce the visibility of the scars. Loosened tiles can be glued down *(opposite, bottom right),* but first determine whether water from leaking plumbing caused them to come adrift; if so, repair the leak before fixing the floor. Shallow scratches in asphalt and vinyl-asbestos floors can be sanded down with a very fine sandpaper, then waxed. If the floor is vinyl or rubber, gently rub the

scratch lengthwise with the rim of an old coin. This will press the edges of the scratch together so only a thin line remains. Cuts in vinyl or linoleum can be closed with a hot iron *(page 30).*

Small holes in vinyl, linoleum or cork floors can be filled with homemade putty *(Steps 1 and 2).* Holes in asphalt, rubber and vinyl-asbestos cannot be filled, and neither can large holes or tears in any resilient flooring. The best remedy for a tile that is badly damaged is a replacement *(opposite, bottom left);* the best remedy for badly damaged sheet flooring is a patch *(page 30).*

If you do not have spare matching tiles or sheet flooring and cannot buy any, look for replacements in inconspicuous areas of your floor—under a refrigerator or at the back of a closet. Remove the desired tile or section from the hidden area and replace it with a nonmatching material of equal thickness, using the techniques employed for replacing a damaged tile or patching damaged sheet flooring *(page 30);* take special care not to break the piece you are removing. (It is almost impossible to remove cork without destroying it, but cork tiles usually can be matched from a dealer's stock.)

Two basic types of adhesive are used when repairing resilient floors: water-based latex adhesive and solvent-based

adhesive. Because latex can be applied in thin coats with a paintbrush and clings firmly to other adhesives, it is the best for recementing loose tiles and for gluing down blisters in sheet flooring *(page 31).* Solvent-based adhesives are thicker, can be applied with a notched trowel and should be used when replacing whole tiles or sections of sheet flooring. Caution: solvent-based adhesives are highly flammable and give off noxious fumes; use them only in rooms that are well ventilated, turn off pilot lights before starting and keep adhesive containers tightly closed when they are not in use.

There are several kinds of solvent-based adhesives. Which you use will depend on the type of resilient flooring and the surface on which it is laid—wood, concrete, ceramic tiles, hardboard, felt or an older resilient floor. Give your floor dealer detailed information so he can prescribe the correct adhesive.

If your resilient floor is glued to an asphalt-felt underlayment, you may tear the felt while removing damaged flooring. If so, glue the felt together with latex adhesive and allow it to dry before continuing the job. If the felt is too badly torn to stick together, glue down enough layers of replacement felt to maintain the same floor level. Use 15-pound asphalt felt and thin latex adhesive.

Filling Small Holes

1 Mixing the putty. To make a paste filler for vinyl or linoleum, fold a spare piece of the flooring with the top surface on the outside and scrape along the fold with a utility knife, catching the powdery flakes in a bowl. Refold the material as you wear down the surface and continue scraping until the bowl contains what appears to be more than enough powder to fill the hole. Then add a few drops of clear nail polish, stirring with a small stick until the mixture is the consistency of putty.

To make putty for cork flooring, scrape a bottle cork and mix the shavings with clear shellac.

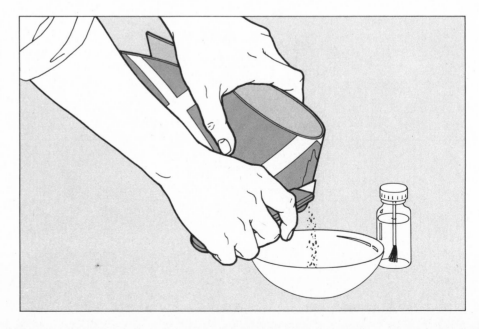

2 Filling the hole. To protect the undamaged floor, surround the hole with a border of masking tape at least an inch wide and then force the filler firmly into the hole with a putty knife. Scrape off the excess and smooth the surface of the patch with the knife. Let the paste set for 30 minutes; then remove the masking tape and buff the patch with 00-grade steel wool. If the repaired area is duller than the surrounding floor, brush a thin coat of clear nail polish on it.

Replacing a Damaged Tile

Removing a tile. For vinyl-asbestos or asphalt flooring, lay a towel on the tile and warm it with an iron set at medium heat until the adhesive softens and you can lift one corner with a putty knife. Pull up the corner while you slice at the adhesive underneath with the putty knife, reheating the tile with the iron if necessary, until you can remove the entire tile. Wait for the adhesive remaining on the subfloor to harden—allow about an hour—then scrape it up.

To remove a damaged vinyl or rubber tile, chip it out with a hammer and chisel, starting at the center. If you are removing a good vinyl or rubber tile you plan to reuse, pry up one edge with a chisel and gently chip through adhesive beneath the tile. Scrape up old adhesive.

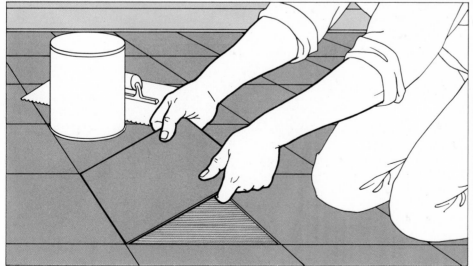

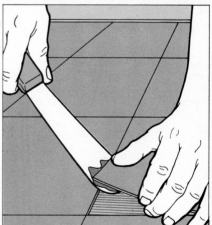

Installing a replacement. Spread a thin layer of solvent-based adhesive—not more than half the thickness of your tile—on the subfloor with a notched trowel, then butt one edge of the new tile against the edge of an adjoining tile, aligning the pattern. Ease the tile into place. Make sure it is level with surrounding tiles; if it is too high, press it down and quickly wipe up excess adhesive before it dries; if the tile is too low, pull it up and add more adhesive beneath it. Then put a 20-pound weight on it for the time specified by the adhesive manufacturer.

Securing a loose tile. Lift the loose portion of the tile and spread a thin coat of latex adhesive on the underside with a narrow, flexible spatula. If only a corner of the tile is unstuck, loosen more of it until you can turn the tile back far enough to spread the adhesive. Press the tile into place, making it level with surrounding tiles, and hold it down with a 20-pound weight for at least an hour.

Patching Sheet Flooring

1 Cutting the patch. Tape a piece of flooring over the damaged area, aligning its design with that on the floor. With a metal straightedge and a utility knife, score the patching material in the shape of the patch you want, following lines in the design wherever possible. Using the scored line as a guide, cut through the replacement material and the floor covering underneath. Keep slicing along the same lines until you have cut through both sheets. Clear away the floor and loosen the adhesive under the section you are replacing (*page 29*). Remove the section and scrape out old adhesive.

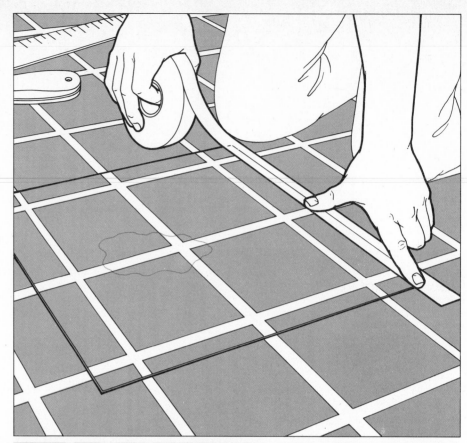

2 Installing the patch. Spread adhesive over the exposed subfloor and set in the replacement patch as you would a tile (*page 29*). Then hide the outline of the patch by covering its edges with heavy aluminum foil, dull side down, and pressing the foil several times with a very hot iron (*inset*). This process, which also can be used to seal deep scratches in linoleum or solid vinyl, will partly melt the cut edges of the flooring so they form a solid and almost undetectable bond.

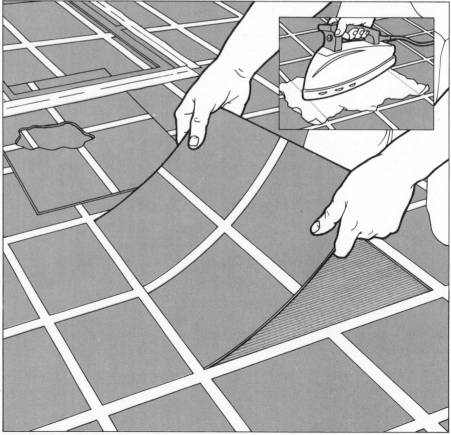

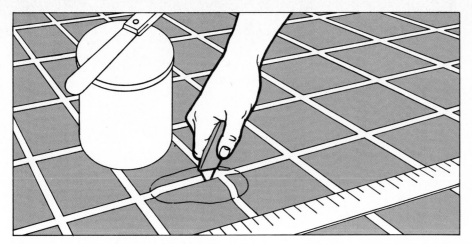

Flattening Bulges in Linoleum

Deflating a blister. Score, then slice, along the length of a blister with a utility knife, extending the cut ½ inch beyond the blister at both ends. Try to cut along a line in the linoleum pattern to make the repair less conspicuous. With a spatula, spread a thin layer of latex adhesive through the slit onto the underside of the flooring. Press the linoleum down; if one edge overlaps because the flooring has stretched, use it as a guide to trim the edge beneath. Remove trimmed-off scrap, then press the edges together and put a 20-pound weight on the repaired area for at least one hour.

Keeping That Resilient Beauty

The basic maxim for keeping a resilient floor clean and shiny is: less is better. Many people think a resilient floor needs a weekly scrubbing, then a coat of glossy polish. This regimen is unnecessarily hard on the householder and not particularly good for the floor—too much washing can loosen the adhesive. With modern materials, polishing is rarely necessary. Most contemporary resilient flooring has a permanent finish that not only is as hard, smooth and shiny as wax but also functions as wax is supposed to: its tough film guards the floor against stains and dirt.

How often your floor should be cleaned depends on the material it is made of—some are more resistant to dirt than others *(page 46)*—and the traffic it bears. But the general rule of less is better is always applicable: do not polish when wet-mopping is sufficient; do not wet-mop when damp-mopping will do; do not damp-mop when a good sweeping is enough.

Restraint with the scrub brush is particularly important when you are caring for a newly installed or recently repaired floor. Do not wash it for at least four days after the job is done, to give the adhesive time to form a solid bond. Then remove dirt with a damp mop or cloth and carefully scrape up spots of adhesive with a putty knife.

For regular cleaning, a good daily sweeping plus an occasional damp-mopping is normally sufficient to remove dust and dirt. If you think your floor really needs washing with detergent and water, avoid doing it more often than every three to six weeks.

However, even so-called permanent finishes eventually dull with age and wear. If you insist on a high-gloss finish, you can restore one to old flooring with water-based floor polish in thin coats. To prevent discoloration, take off the polish once or twice a year with commercial wax remover and steel wool.

The tough finishes that normally eliminate the need for polish also protect new resilient floors against stains from substances ranging from spilled food to splashed paint. Even so, you should quickly soak up any spillage and wash the area. If stains remain, they can generally be removed by a cleaner suited to the stain substance. Caution: some of the chemicals used give off noxious fumes and can irritate skin, so work in a well-ventilated room and wear rubber gloves to protect your hands. The following treatments are recommended for stains caused by common substances:

☐ Alcoholic beverages: rub the spot with a cloth that has been dampened with rubbing alcohol.

☐ Blood: sponge with cold water; if that does not work, sponge with a solution of 1 part ammonia to 9 parts water.

☐ Candle wax, chewing gum and tar: cover with a plastic bag filled with ice cubes. When the material becomes brittle, scrape it off with a plastic spatula.

☐ Candy: rub with liquid detergent and grade 00 steel wool unless the floor is a "waxless" vinyl; in that case use a plastic scouring pad, warm water and powdered detergent.

☐ Cigarette burns: rub with scouring powder and grade 00 steel wool.

☐ Coffee and canned or frozen juice: cover for several hours with a cloth saturated in a solution of 1 part glycerine (available at drugstores) to 3 parts water. If the stain remains, rub it gently with scouring powder on a damp cloth.

☐ Fresh fruit: wearing rubber gloves, rub with a cloth dampened with a solution of 1 tablespoon oxalic acid, a powerful—and toxic—solvent available at hardware stores, and 1 pint water.

☐ Grease and oil: remove as much as possible with paper towels, then wash the stain with a cloth dampened in liquid detergent and warm water.

☐ Mustard or urine: cover for several hours with a cloth soaked in 3 to 5 per cent hydrogen peroxide (available in drugstores) and cover that cloth with another soaked in household ammonia.

☐ Paint or varnish: rub with grade 00 steel wool dipped in warm water and liquid detergent.

☐ Leather and rubber scuff marks: scrub with a cloth soaked in a solution of 1 part ammonia to 9 parts water.

☐ Shoe or nail polish: rub with grade 00 steel wool that has been soaked in warm water and scouring powder.

Some Easy Repairs for Hard-surfaced Floors

The hard flooring materials—concrete and marble, slate or ceramic tiles—are the most durable. They are also the most inflexible and brittle. All of them can be cracked by the fall of a heavy weight from above. If they are inadequately supported from below, they can be pulled apart by normal expansion and contraction in the supporting framework of a house. Under this invisible but constant stress, tiles will loosen and break; concrete will crumble and crack.

A tile floor that is cracked throughout a room is usually a sign of trouble in the structure beneath it. You may have to replace the entire floor by clearing out the old tile, tightening the subfloor (pages 8-10) and laying new tile.

Ceramic tiles are generally laid in an organic or thin-set adhesive if the subfloor is wood, using the procedures on pages 52-55. Slate and marble, as well as ceramic over concrete, are generally laid in mortar. When only a few tiles are cracked your job is easier—replace the tiles, one by one, using one of a number of flexible adhesives to simplify the job. Use organic adhesives for replacements laid directly on a wood subfloor or on smooth, dry concrete. To replace tiles on damp, damaged or irregular mortar beds, use epoxy adhesives consisting of resins and hardeners that must be mixed together before application.

A new tile must be regrouted preferably with silicone grout, which comes premixed in squeeze tubes, cures quickly and adheres to both old and new tile. Silicone grouts come in a variety of colors; you can match the grout already in place or even replace all the grout with a new color to give a fresh look to an old tile floor. The techniques shown on these pages illustrate a professional's way of replacing an irregular tile at the base of a fixture or pipe on a ceramic tile floor. Replacing marble or slate tile involves only slight variations in procedure.

Like the flexible adhesives that simplify repairs to tile floors, recently developed materials make it easy to patch concrete. Cracks less than an inch wide can be filled with a premixed vinyl or latex patching compound. Larger cracks can be repaired by using premixed concrete and special bonding agents. At one time, the most skilled craftsman could not guarantee a large concrete patch. The dry concrete around the patch absorbed water from the new concrete so the new material could not form a bond with the old. The patch cracked because it could not cure without water. But an epoxy bonding agent applied to the old concrete just before the patch is made (page 34), prevents water loss. And the patch itself, reinforced with wire mesh, can be given flexibility with premixed patching concretes. Even if a concrete slab settles slightly, the patch will not crack.

After patching the concrete, you can restore the appearance of the floor or give the floor a completely new look with paint (page 35). Here, too, modern materials make a difference: new paints, especially formulated for concrete and available in a variety of colors and textures, resist blistering and peeling.

A Tight Fit around a Fixture

1 **Removing the grout.** Wearing protective glasses, use a small cold chisel and hammer to chip out the grout at the edges of a damaged ceramic tile. Make a hole in each line of grout by striking a small cold chisel straight down, then angle the chisel to 45° and chip outward from the hole. Caution: tap the chisel lightly; heavy blows can cause cracks in the surrounding tiles. Use a wire brush to clean out any excess grout.

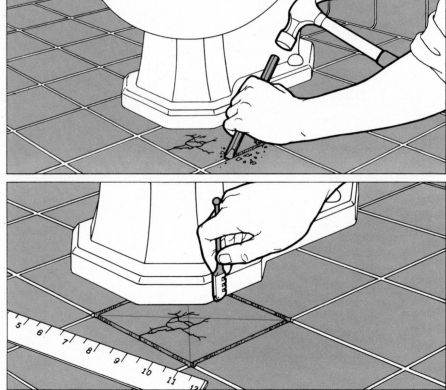

2 **Taking out the tile.** Score an X in ceramic tile from corner to corner, then along the base of the fixture, using a straightedge and glass cutter. Drill a hole through the center of the X with a ¼-inch masonry bit. Hammer a cold chisel into the hole and, working toward the edges, break the tile into small pieces. Clean out the fragments of tile and scrape the old adhesive beneath them with a putty knife. On a marble or slate tile, mark an X with a grease pencil and drill ¾-inch holes ½ inch apart along the X and into the tile along the base of the fixture, using a masonry bit. Then break out the tile with a hammer and cold chisel.

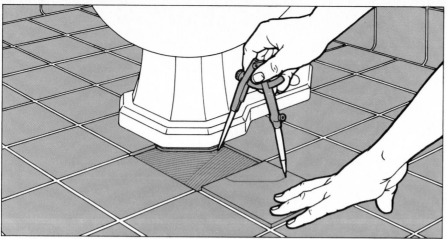

3 **Marking the new tile.** Set a new tile over the tile adjacent to the space you have cleared. Replace the pencil in a school compass—or scribe (*page 51, Step 3*)—with a grease pencil and open it to span the width of a single tile, then set the pencil at the edge of the new tile and the point of the scribe at the corresponding point on the base of the fixture. Steady the tile with one hand and move the scribe slowly along the base of the fixture with the other until the pencil has marked the shape of the base on the new tile.

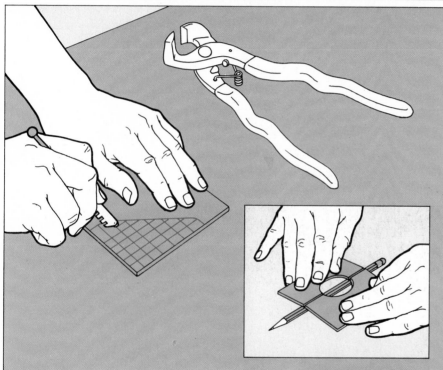

4 **Cutting the tile.** Using a glass cutter, score the line you have marked on ceramic tile, then score a crisscross pattern over the area to be cut away. Snip ⅛-inch pieces of tile away from the scored area with tile nippers. Angle the nippers so that you use only the corners of its blades; otherwise, the tile may break. Check the fit of the tile and smooth the edges with an emery cloth. To cut a marble or slate tile, use a saber saw fitted with a tungsten carbide blade or a hacksaw fitted with a tungsten carbide rod saw.

A replacement for a tile around a pipe is easier to make. Measure the diameter of the pipe and drill a hole of the same size in the tile using a carbide-tipped hole saw. On marble or slate, mark the hole for the pipe on the tile, drill a starter hole at the center, and, using a saber saw fitted with a tungsten carbide blade, cut out the pipe hole. Score the tile from the pipe hole to the edges, using a glass cutter for ceramic or a circular saw and masonry blade for marble or slate. Set the tile over a pencil on a flat surface and press down on both sides until it breaks (*inset*). Smooth the edges with an emery cloth.

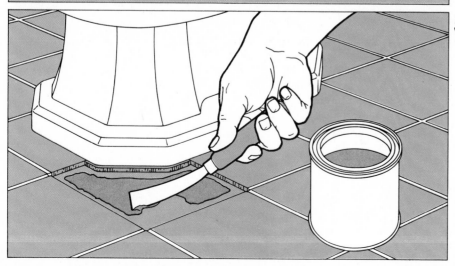

5 **Setting the tile in place.** Using a putty knife, spread adhesive over the exposed subfloor or mortar bed; use organic adhesive on a dry, smooth surface, epoxy adhesive on one that is moist or uneven. If the new tile has tabs on its back, spread the adhesive over the bottom of the tile, covering the tabs completely, and leave the border uncovered so that the adhesive does not ooze out when you press the tile in place. In either case, apply enough adhesive to raise the tile slightly higher than the ones around it. Use toothpicks or coins set on edge as spacers to keep the joints between ceramic tiles open and even; marble and slate tiles normally butt tightly against each other. Then, lay a 2-by-4 across the tile and tap it down with a hammer.

Let the adhesive set for 24 hours, remove the spacers and fill the joints with silicone grout.

Durable Patches
for a Concrete Floor

1 Preparing the area. Wearing gloves and goggles, break the damaged concrete into small, easily carried pieces with a sledge or an electric jackhammer (page 18) and clear away the debris. Use a cold chisel and a hammer to angle the exposed edges of the slab toward the center of the hole you have made; roughen the edges of the slab with a wire brush and remove loose particles of concrete. Dig 4 inches below the bottom of the slab. Tamp the dirt inside the hole with the end of a 2-by-4 and fill the hole to the bottom of the slab with clean ¾-inch gravel.

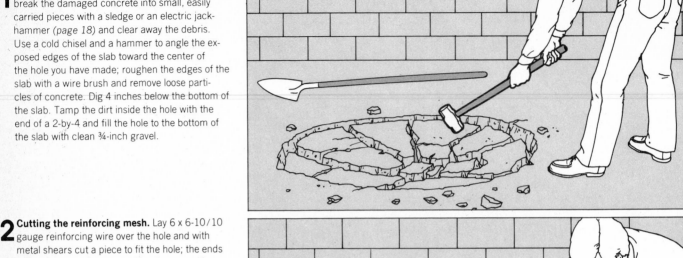

2 Cutting the reinforcing mesh. Lay 6 x 6-10/10 gauge reinforcing wire over the hole and with metal shears cut a piece to fit the hole; the ends of the wires should rest against the exposed edges of the concrete slab. Reinforcing wire usually comes in rolls 5 feet wide; if you need a patch that is wider than 5 feet, join two strips of wire by twisting the free strands together. Set two bricks under the wire to keep it centered between the top and bottom of the hole when the new concrete is poured.

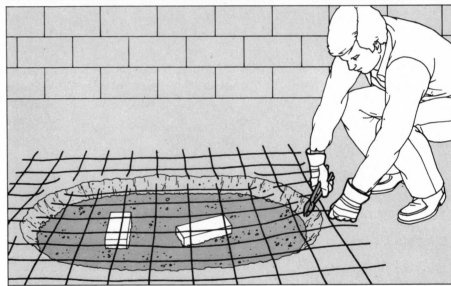

3 Pouring the patch. Form a cone of premixed patching concrete on a piece of plywood, hollow out the top and pour water into the center as specified by the manufacturer. Mix them together with a shovel until the concrete is firm but workable. Coat the edges of the hole with an epoxy bonding agent. Before the coating dries, shovel the concrete into the hole, jabbing into it to force it against the sides of the hole and under the reinforcing wire. Fill the hole to the level of the slab, then add a few extra shovels of concrete to allow for settling and shrinking. With a rake, pull the wire about halfway up to the surface of the concrete at all points, but be sure that none of the wire is exposed.

4 **Finishing the patch.** With a helper, sweep a straight 2-by-4 across the surface of the patch to level it, working the board back and forth as you sweep. If you find depressions in the surface, fill them with concrete and go over the patch again with the 2-by-4. A thin film of water will soon appear on the surface. When it evaporates and the surface sheen disappears, smooth the patch with a metal trowel *(page 61, Step 5)*. If the patch is too large to trowel from its edges, kneel on boards laid across it and work backward from one side of the patch to the other, moving the boards as you go.

When the concrete hardens, sprinkle it with water and cover it with polyethylene to prevent moisture from escaping. Let the patch cure for three to seven days, checking it every day to be sure it is damp, and sprinkling it with water if needed.

Cosmetics for Concrete

A raw concrete floor has a certain rough beauty, but no one likes a stained floor and most people prefer one finished with a sealer or a paint. To remove stains or to paint, you must match materials and methods to your situation.

Most stains can be scrubbed away with a household detergent, but deep stains may require special treatment. Fold a piece of cheesecloth several times and lay it over the stained area. Then, pour one of the chemicals listed below over the cloth. The chemicals will dissolve the stain, and the cheese-cloth will absorb the chemicals. Use the following recipes for specific stains:

☐ Rust: use 1 part sodium citrate to 6 parts glycerin.

☐ Copper, bronze or ink: use 1 part ammonia to 9 parts water.

☐ Grease, oil or mildew: use 1 pound trisodium phosphate to 1 gallon water.

☐ Iron: use 1 part oxalic acid to 9 parts water.

☐ Old paint: use a commercial paint remover.

Penetrating sealers are the least expensive and simplest finishes for concrete. They can be easily applied, dry in about eight hours and leave a thin film that protects against minor stains.

Until recently, concrete floors had to be specially prepared for painting, because concrete contains alkalies that make most paints blister and peel. To neutralize the alkalies, the floors were treated with a strong solution of muriatic acid, difficult and somewhat dangerous to apply. The paints listed below can be used on an untreated concrete floor after a suitable waiting period. All can be spatter-dashed—a technique that obscures small stains in concrete and creates a decorative effect *(left)*.

Epoxy-polyurethane coatings can be applied about a month after the concrete is poured. They are relatively expensive but more durable than other types. Most come ready to apply but a few manufacturers make "two-pot" coatings, for which resins and hardeners must be premixed. Epoxy-polyurethanes usually need two coats; a few types need a primer. Most dry in about six hours to a clear, tough, glossy finish.

Solvent-thinned, rubber-based paints, which are not as long lasting as epoxy-polyurethanes, are more water resistant; they can be applied to damp surfaces and are suited to humid areas. You will need three coats, the first applied two months after the concrete is poured. The paint dries in one half to four hours and the job can be done in a day. The paint solvents are noxious: always work in a well-ventilated room.

Latex paints especially designed for concrete are cheaper than rubber-based or epoxy-polyurethane paints. Because they are water based, application and cleanup are easy, but they are far less durable than the others and can be damaged by freezing; do not use them on heavily trafficked areas or where sudden drops in temperature are common. Apply three coats, beginning two months after the concrete is poured.

To spatter-dash a floor, apply two coats of paint. Before you apply the third and contrasting coat *(left)*, mask the walls with newspaper and wear goggles, gloves and a hat. Load a brush with the paint and strike the handle, heel or bristles against the edge of a 1-by-2 board. Practice the technique over a sheet of paper before you begin.

2

New Floors: A Wealth of Choices

Laying a new wood floor. A power-nailing machine makes easy work of installing finished oak tongue-and-groove flooring. When struck with a five-pound rubber-headed mallet, the machine drives 2-inch flooring cleats into the tongue of a board, fastening it securely to the subfloor. The sheets of asphalt-felt paper opposite, laid between the flooring and the subfloor to deaden sound (page 41), are chalked to locate joists underneath.

A century or so ago the very rich walked on terrazzo or marble, but the most common flooring materials, at least in North America, were wood planks, rough stones or dirt. Synthetics and modern industry changed all that. In 1863 a Briton named Frederick Walton invented a new kind of flooring—linoleum, made by mixing linseed oil, ground-up cork and natural resins. It was inexpensive, impervious to most spills and colorfully decorated with built-in patterns, and its popularity inspired the development of other man-made resilient floors of asphalt, rubber and plastic resins. Over the same period, mass production and modern transportation put floors of traditional materials that had been prohibitively expensive—wood parquet, ceramic tile, even marble—within the reach of millions of people.

Now when installing a new floor you can select the material best suited to the demands of a particular room. Durability and economy of upkeep can govern the choice for a workroom while appearance and comfort determine what will go underfoot in living room or den. Wood, the traditional floor covering, is still the most versatile. Usually consisting of nailed oak strips or parquet blocks that are fastened down with adhesive, hardwood flooring is easy to walk on and is practical for most areas except the "wet rooms." Wood floors, while more expensive than resilient tiles or sheet flooring, last longer and provide a feeling of warmth that synthetic tiles lack. Wood-strip and parquet floors also supply an extra layer of insulation, and a new wood floor nailed to an existing floor or subfloor reinforces the structure of the house. Hardwood floors are likely to shrink and swell with changes in moisture, but when the boards are installed in a reasonably dry area they will last as long as your home.

In kitchens and playrooms, the synthetic floorings that began with Frederick Walton's linoleum are the most popular. They are called resilient because they cushion the impact of feet or dropped objects. They come either as tiles that can be installed in a variety of designs (pages 46-49), or in rolled sheets that can be cut to fit irregularly shaped rooms (pages 50-51). In potentially damp areas, such as entryways or bathrooms, ceramic tiles, flagstones or marble surpass both wood and resilient materials in durability and water protection. Flagstones must be set in concrete. Marble or ceramic tiles can be laid on a concrete base prepared with a thin bed of mortar, or on a plywood subfloor by means of adhesives (page 52).

In garages, basements and workrooms, you can create a good floor simply by pouring one of concrete (pages 56-63). Concrete can serve as a base for finished flooring, can be left bare, or can be coated with paints for a heavy-duty surface that seals out grease and stains and will last for years with little more care than an occasional sweeping.

Getting a Room Ready for a New Wood Floor

Laying a new wood floor is often easier and less time-consuming than laying many of the so-called quick and easy floor coverings of synthetic sheet or tile. Wood, unlike most resilient materials, does not require a smooth, carefully prepared surface. In most cases, you use the existing floor or a plywood subfloor covered with strips of asphalt-felt building paper. A new subfloor is probably unnecessary if you have old wood or resilient flooring in reasonably good shape. In this case, drive down raised nails, renail loose boards and replace badly warped ones *(pages 11-13)*, and cement down loose tiles or torn sheeting *(pages 29-31)*.

If you suspect the old floor may conceal damage or decay, check underneath it. Remove damaged flooring and subflooring and patch the hole with plywood equal to the thickness of the old finished floor. If the damage is extensive,

remove the entire floor, check for and repair any structural damage *(pages 14-23)*, then lay a new plywood subfloor. Before trying to floor over concrete, check for excess dampness by laying a 16-inch square of heavy plastic over the slab and sealing the edges with tape. If drops of water have condensed on the plastic after several days, the concrete is a poor choice for a finished wood floor.

If the concrete is suitable, provide a moisture barrier for the new floor by covering the slab with polyethylene film sandwiched between two layers of 1-by-2 sleepers *(opposite)*. Then lay a plywood subfloor on the sleepers.

A ceramic-tile floor makes an unstable base for a new wood floor. Nailing tongue-and-groove flooring on top of ceramic tiles will loosen and crack the tiles—even if they are covered with plywood. Remove old tiles and install a new

subfloor before you lay strip flooring.

To install a new subfloor or replace a damaged old one, use C-D grade plywood at least ⅝ inch thick. Check the joists underneath before laying subflooring, and if they are more than 16 inches apart, or are made of lumber smaller than 2-by-8, reinforce them *(pages 16-17)*, or install new joists in the spaces between the old ones. In rooms like attics, where small joists may cover long spans, it may be necessary to increase the thickness of the plywood subfloor to ¾ inch.

Always lay plywood subflooring with the outer grain perpendicular to the joists, and stagger the sheets so that the joints do not align. Where two sheets meet at a joist, trim them so that there is a bearing surface for both, and leave ⅛-inch spaces at the sides and 1/16-inch spaces at the ends to allow room for expansion of the subfloor.

Laying a new subfloor. Apply a ¼-inch bead of subfloor construction adhesive in a serpentine pattern to each joist or sleeper. Spread only enough adhesive to lay one or two sheets at a time. Before the adhesive sets, lay the plywood on top of the joists and nail down each sheet with eightpenny ringed or coated nails sold for this purpose. Stagger the nails and space them 6 inches apart, ⅜ inch from the edges at end joints. Space the nails 10 inches apart between the ends of the sheets.

If the two outer joists in the room are hidden beneath walls, install cleats *(inset)* to provide a bearing surface for the outer subfloor sheets. Nail two 2-by-4s to each hidden joist. Then screw the 2-by-4s into the joists with ⅜-inch lag screws, 6 inches long and spaced 16 inches apart.

An Antimoisture Sandwich

1 **Laying bottom sleepers.** Sweep the floor clean and apply a coat of masonry primer. When the primer dries, snap chalk lines 16 inches apart at right angles to the long dimension of the room. Cover each line with a 2-inch-wide ribbon of either a synthetic rubber-based adhesive or an asphalt mastic designed for bonding wood to concrete. Embed random lengths of pressure-treated 1-by-2s in the adhesive or the mastic, flat side down, leaving about a ½-inch space between ends. Secure the sleepers with 1½-inch concrete nails 24 inches or so apart.

2 **Attaching the top sleepers.** Lay sheets of 4-mil polyethylene film over the sleepers, overlapping joints 6 inches. Nail a second course of 1-by-2s on top of each first course, sandwiching the film between the two layers.

Floating a Floor to Reduce Noise

Uncarpeted wood floors upstairs are noisy. The best way to muffle the sounds of footsteps is to lay carpeting, but for excessively noisy areas, you can adapt the "floating floor" techniques that were developed to soundproof apartment buildings.

To construct a floating floor, staple ½-inch insulation board, available from lumberyards in 4-by-8 sheets, to the existing floor or subfloor. Mark the position of the joists on each sheet and do not staple into any joists. Glue 1-by-3 furring strips to the board with subfloor construction adhesive, placing the strips parallel to one another between joists. Then fasten a ½-inch plywood subfloor to the furring strips (right) and install the finish flooring. You can further muffle airborne noise by laying insulating batts between the open floor joists underneath the subfloor.

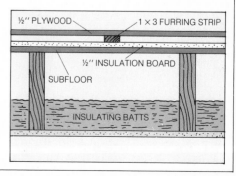

Installing a Wood Floor Board by Board

A floor of oak strip boards—or of the less common hardboards, such as maple, pecan, hickory and ash, that can be found at specialty lumberyards—is durable and elegant in appearance, yet remarkably simple to install. And with the aid of a power nailer, available at tool-rental agencies, the job goes fast.

Flooring boards that are of conventional hardwood are ¾ inch thick and 2 to 4 inches wide. The boards are milled with interlocking tongues and grooves on their sides and ends, and can be blind-nailed through their tongues *(page 12),* a technique that makes the joints between boards uniform and hides the nailheads. Broader hardwood planks, which may be as wide as 8 inches, must be screwed into the subfloor as well as blind-nailed to keep them from buckling *(page 45).*

Before they are nailed in place, floorboards are extremely susceptible to warping and swelling caused by moisture. Bring your home to its normal humidity before the wood is delivered: in winter, heat the room adequately, and in summer keep the air conditioner running. Insist that hardwood flooring be delivered on a dry day, at least three days before you plan to lay your floor. Untie the bundles and stack the boards in loose piles to let them adjust to the humidity and temperature of the room.

When laying the floor, you will have to nail the first few boards by hand before you will have room to use the power nailer for the rest of the floor. The nailer, which consists of a spring-operated mechanism that drives barbed flooring cleats, is triggered by the blows from a rubber-headed mallet. The cleats feed into the nailer like bullets from a clip in an automatic rifle: each blow of the mallet drives home a cleat and simultaneously reloads and cocks the machine. To get the knack of working with the nailer before you use it, practice on a scrap of flooring set atop some spare plywood.

How to Buy Hardwood Flooring

Hardwood flooring—no matter what the wood—is graded according to the standards that are set by the National Oak Flooring Manufacturers Association. The boards are rated in order of decreasing quality as "clear," "select," "No. 1 common" or "No. 2 common," depending on color, grain and imperfections such as knots and streaks.

All strip flooring is sold in random lengths. Individual boards range from 9 to 102 inches long, but the boards are always sold according to a "flooring board foot" formula, based on the premilled size of the boards. To determine the amount of flooring you will need, calculate the area of your room in square feet. If you are buying ¾-by-2¼-inch boards, the most common size, increase the area measurement by 38.3 per cent to convert to flooring board feet and to account for wastage. For example, a 16-by-20-foot room totals 320 square feet. Multiplying 320 by 1.383 gives 443 flooring board feet. For boards of other dimensions, ask your flooring distributor for the proper conversion factor.

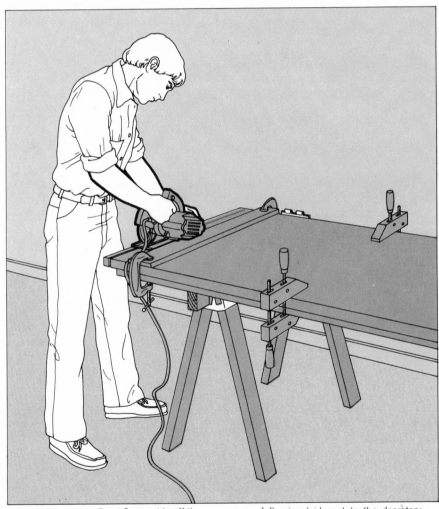

1 **Trimming for a new floor.** Saw a strip off the bottom of each door that opens into a room where you will lay a new wood-strip floor. Use the uncut edge of a piece of plywood as a guide to making a straight cut. To determine the depth of the cut, simulate the new floor with scraps of flooring laid next to the doorstop; include the height of a threshold if you plan to install one. Expose the subfloor and measure up from it to find the new floor height of tiled or carpeted rooms. Finally, mark and cut off the bottoms of the doorstop and doorcasings.

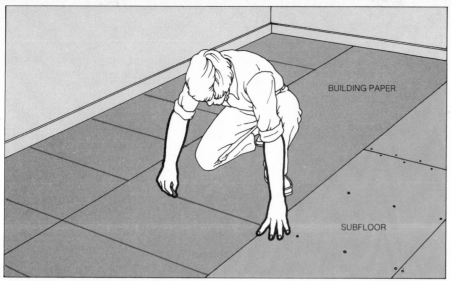

BUILDING PAPER

SUBFLOOR

2 Marking the joists. Unroll strips of 15-pound asphalt-felt building paper across the room and mark on each the positions of the joists. When installing a new wood floor on a plywood subfloor, simply use the subfloor nailing pattern as a guide to the joist positions. If these positions are hidden by existing flooring—and if they cannot be determined from below, as would be the case if you were working above an unfinished basement—drill pilot holes to locate the joists.

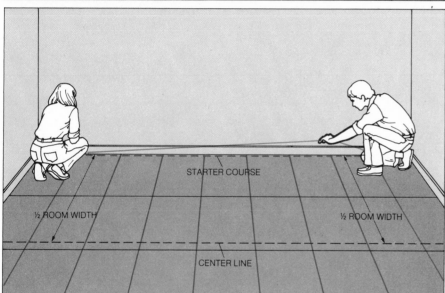

STARTER COURSE

½ ROOM WIDTH   ½ ROOM WIDTH

CENTER LINE

3 Aligning the starter course. Find the midpoints of the walls parallel to the joists and snap a chalk line between them to mark the center of the room. Measure equal distances from the center line to within roughly ½ inch of the end wall and snap a chalk line between the points. Using this line to mark the starter course along the wall will guarantee that the center boards of the room look straight even if the room is not truly square. The gap between the first course and the baseboard will be hidden by the shoe molding.

4 Face-nailing the first course. With a helper, align a long flooring board, tongue out, along the starting chalk line. Drive eightpenny finishing nails through predrilled holes at each end of the board, as near to the grooved edge as possible. Drive additional nails through predrilled holes at every joist and at midpoints between joists. The nailheads will be covered later by shoe molding. In the same way, nail down the other boards to complete the first course.

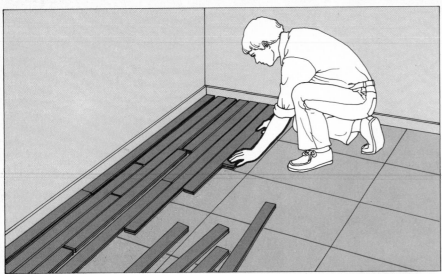

5 **Arranging the field.** Working out from the starter strip, rack seven or eight loose rows of flooring boards in a staggered pattern with end joints in adjoining rows at least 6 inches apart. Find or cut pieces to fit within ½ inch of the end wall. Following the procedure on page 12, jam the boards snug, grooves to tongues, and blind-nail the second and third courses along joist lines.

FLOORING CLEAT

HEAT REGISTER OPENING

6 **Using the power nailer.** Slip the head of the nailing machine onto the tongue of the first board of the fourth course, about 2 inches from the end wall, and thump its plunger with a three-pound rubber-headed mallet to drive a cleat through the tongue of the board and into the subfloor (*inset*). Using your heel to keep the board fitted tightly against the preceding course, drive extra cleats into the tongue at each joist, halfway between joists, and near the board's end. Install as many boards with the nailer as you can, until you get too close to the far wall to use it. Use a claw hammer to pry out cleats that do not penetrate completely. A wood scrap under the hammer will keep it from marring the flooring.

7 **Dressing a board to fit.** To work around openings in the floor, such as heat registers (*inset*), trial-fit boards over the gaps, decide whether the tongue or the groove will be saved, mark and cut them. Clamp the end of the board firmly to a workbench before sawing.

8 **Framing special borders.** Using a miter box, saw boards at 45° angles to frame a fireplace hearth *(inset)*. Rip off the boards' tongues when necessary to make them fit flush to adjoining boards. Face-nail them into place.

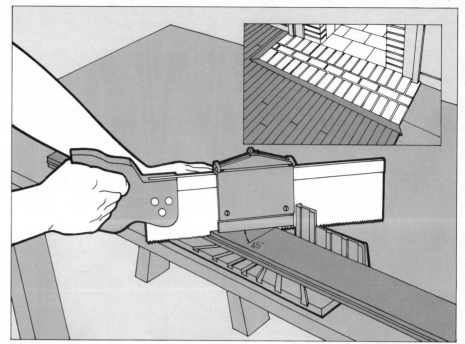

9 **Reversing tongue direction.** To install tongue-and-groove boards in a hall or closet opening onto the groove side of the starting course, join groove to groove with a slip tongue, available in 3-foot lengths from flooring distributors. After placing the slip tongue into the back-to-back grooves, put the nailer's head over the tongue of the loose board and nail it to the floor.

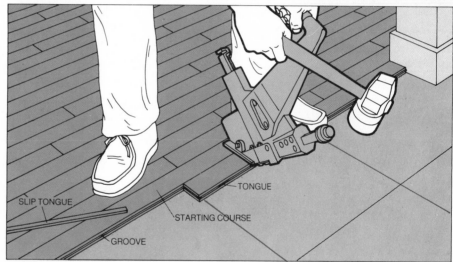

10 **Installing the final boards.** If a gap of more than ½ inch remains at the far wall, dress off the tongue sides of several boards *(Step 7)*, wedge them into the gap and face-nail them into place. To hold them tight for nailing, use your foot to angle a pry bar between the wall and the boards. Slip a scrap of wood between the pry bar and the wall to protect the baseboard.

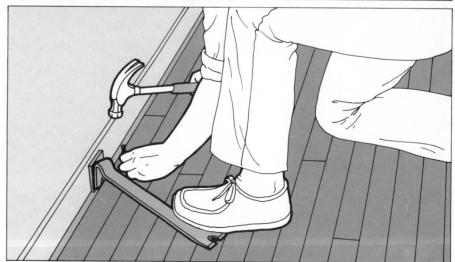

11 **Finishing off a doorway.** Face-nail a clam-shell reducer strip (so called because its rounded top makes it resemble half a clam shell) at a doorway where a new wood floor meets a lower floor. The reducer strip, available at flooring distributors, is milled on one side to fit over the tongue of an adjoining board. The strip can also be butted to the ends of floorboards that run at right angles to a doorway.

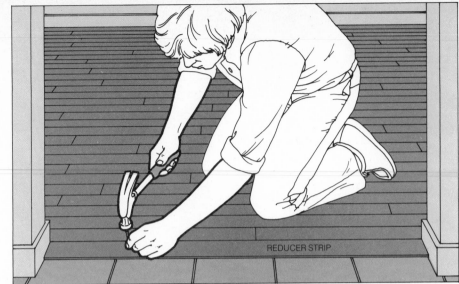

REDUCER STRIP

12 **Laying expansion strips.** Wedge strips of ¾-inch corkboard into the space where the floor meets glass sliding doors, ceramic tiles or a laid stone floor. The cork acts as a cushion that compresses or expands to compensate for shrinkage or swelling of the floorboards.

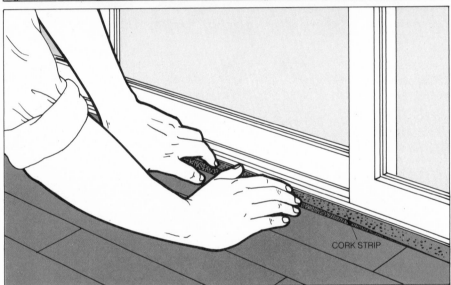

CORK STRIP

13 **Installing shoe molding.** Fasten ¾-inch shoe molding over the gap between the flooring and the baseboard with fourpenny finishing nails. Drive the nails horizontally through the middle of the molding into the baseboard to allow the new floor to shrink or expand without tearing the shoe molding.

Screws to Hold
a Wide Plank Floor

Drilling the fastening holes. Use a ¾-inch spade bit to drill partly through the ends of the planks. A piece of masking tape on the bit, ¼ inch from the squared end of the spade portion, will serve as a sighting guide for the depth of the hole. Stagger additional screw holes at 20-inch intervals along the faces of long boards.

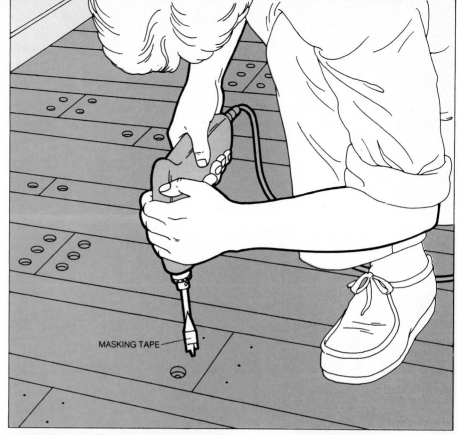

MASKING TAPE

Securing the planks. Drive 1½-inch, No. 6 flathead wood screws through the planks. Then cover the screwheads with hardwood plugs ¼ inch deep and ¾ inch in diameter, bought from a flooring distributor or cut from a length of ¾-inch hardwood dowel. Use white water-base glue to hold the plugs.

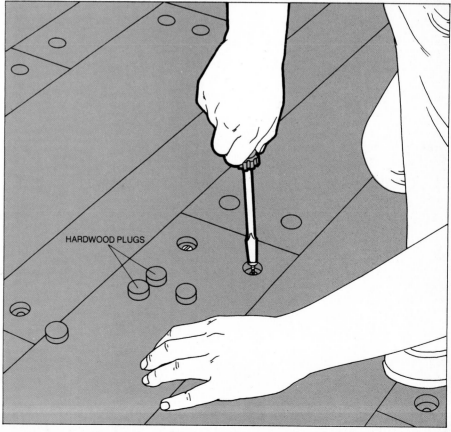

HARDWOOD PLUGS

Eye-catching Patterns in Sheet and Tile

Resilient flooring, sturdy and easy to care for, comes both in sheets, which usually are preferred for kitchens *(page 50)*, and in tiles 9 or 12 inches square. The tiles lend themselves to imaginative design and are available in a variety of materials *(below)*. Wood tile, often called parquet, is installed in much the same way as resilient tile *(page 49)* and also can provide variations in pattern. Choose tiles according to the amount of traffic they will bear and the floor design you have in mind.

You can lay a tile floor all in one color, of course, but once you know how to design a floor you can use tiles to hide visual defects—stripes running across the width make a narrow room look broader, for example—or to define areas of the room, or to decorate your floor with any design that strikes your fancy.

Begin by measuring your room and calculating the number of 9- or 12-inch tiles you will need; then draw the floor on graph paper *(opposite, top)* and work out the design you want by filling squares representing tiles of different colors.

Resilient tile can be laid on almost any surface except strip flooring, which shifts too much to provide a firm base. Cover a strip floor with a ½-inch hardboard or plywood underlayment *(page 30)*. You can lay a new resilient tile floor over an old one if you remove wax and other finishes and repair indentations, holes or loose tiles *(pages 28-31)*.

If you want to lay tile on concrete, check the slab for moisture *(page 38)*, as the combination of dampness and alkali deposits in the concrete will make the tile buckle. If there is moisture on the floor, do not lay resilient tile on the concrete; install a moisture-resistant underlayment first *(page 38)*. If the concrete passes the moisture test, remove paint and stain, repair any cracks or holes *(pages 34-35)*, flatten bumps with a rented electric concrete-grinder, and fill in depressions with a cement-sand-epoxy compound called flash patch, available at hardware stores. Then coat the slab with a clear waterproofing solution, also available at hardware stores and applied with a roller or brush.

After you have made your design and prepared your floor, set up guidelines by the method shown opposite, center. Tiles are laid either on the square, with their edges parallel to the walls, or on the diagonal, with their edges at a 45° angle to the walls; the guidelines you make will ensure that they are correctly aligned in either direction. Then test your plot by making a dry run of tiles *(opposite, bottom)* so that you can adjust your borders and avoid the tedious business of cutting tiny pieces of tile to fit along a wall. If you are trying a complex design you may want to do a dry run over the entire floor.

Once you have tested your design with a dry run, laying the floor is largely a matter of setting tiles in adhesive—your floor dealer can tell you which to use. Most resilient tiles require solvent-based adhesives. Wood tiles, which are laid by a similar process, need a more viscous mastic, either solvent based or latex based. Caution: solvent-based adhesives are flammable; keep the room well ventilated and extinguish any flame before starting. The adhesives work best when the room is warmer than 70°.

Ceramic-tile floors are planned like resilient ones; they are best laid in mortar but can be set in water-resistant organic adhesive. The tiles often have lugs on their edges, creating gaps that must be filled with grout *(pages 52-53)*.

Selecting the Right Adhesive Flooring

Material	Form	Advantages	Limitations
Asphalt	Tile	Least expensive tile; durable; excellent water resistance	Poor resistance to stains and dents; cracks easily; limited availability
Cork	Tile	Most resilient flooring; deadens sounds	Wears rapidly; poor resistance to heavy loads; stains badly unless coated with vinyl
Linoleum	Sheet	Inexpensive; durable; easily cleaned; good grease resistance	Damaged by moisture; requires waxing; limited availability
Rubber	Tile	Very resilient; resists dents; quiet; waterproof	Slippery when wet; poor resistance to grease; requires frequent polishing to maintain gloss
Vinyl	Tile, sheet	Outstanding durability; fine resistance to stains, dents; deadens sound; easy maintenance; variety of colors and patterns	Relatively expensive; poor resistance to burns
Vinyl-asbestos	Tile	Durable; stain-resistant; inexpensive; widely available	Not as resilient or quiet as vinyl
Wood	Tile, block	High wear resistance; rich appearance	Expensive; more difficult to install than most tiles; stains easily; requires more maintenance

Creating the Design

Planning on paper. On graph paper, plot a design for a floor laid on the square *(near right)* or on the diagonal *(far right)*, letting each block represent one tile. If you plan to use 9- rather than 12-inch tiles, multiply the dimensions of the room by 1.33 to find how many tiles to plot to a side. For example, if you use 12-inch tiles, the 20-foot-square design *(near right)* requires 20 per side. If 9-inch tiles are used, it requires 26.6 per side, but plot it for 27: always count fractions of tiles as whole tiles.

Order as many 12-inch tiles as there are square feet in the room. The number of 9-inch tiles you need will equal the number of square feet in the room multiplied by 1.78. For two colors of tile, count the squares of one color and subtract from the total to see how many tiles you need in each; add 5 per cent for waste and repairs.

Guidelines for the dry run. Divide the room into equal quadrants with two chalked strings stretched between nails set at the midpoints of both pairs of opposing walls. Make sure the strings form 90° angles at their intersection by measuring from the intersection 3 feet on one string and 4 feet on the other. The diagonal between the 3- and 4-foot points should measure exactly 5 feet. Do not snap the chalk lines yet.

If your pattern is to be laid on the diagonal, measure the shorter guideline from the intersection to the wall, then set nails into the wall at points that distance to either side of the guideline nail. Repeat this on the opposite wall and stretch chalked strings diagonally between the nails *(inset)* so that they bisect the angles formed by the original guidelines.

Making a dry run. For a pattern laid on the square, lay dry tiles in one quadrant, starting from the intersection and duplicating the colors plotted on your graph paper. If the dry run ends more than half a tile from the walls, snap both chalk lines and remove them. If the last tiles are less than half a tile's width from the wall, move the rows to make larger gaps so you will not have to cut and lay small pieces. Set the chalk lines in the new place and snap them.

To check a diagonal pattern, lay dry tiles point to point along the perpendicular lines defining one quadrant and lay an extra row along the diagonal guideline *(inset)*. When laying a checkerboard pattern, you will achieve the best effect if the floor ends at each wall in a saw-tooth line of half tiles. Add a border of tiles set on the square wide enough to make the diagonally laid field end in a sawtooth; if differences in the widths of borders on two adjacent walls are disturbing, make the borders at least two tiles wide.

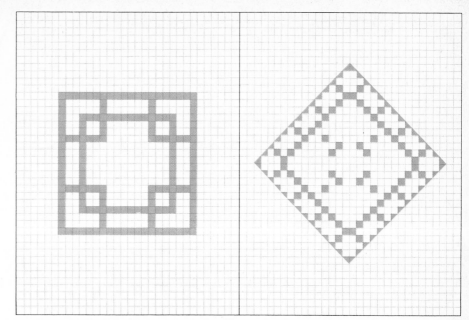

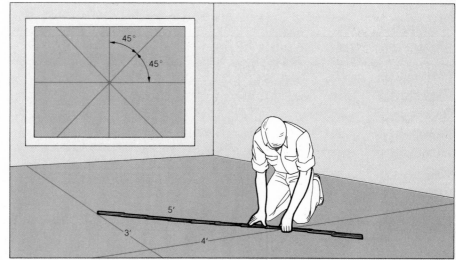

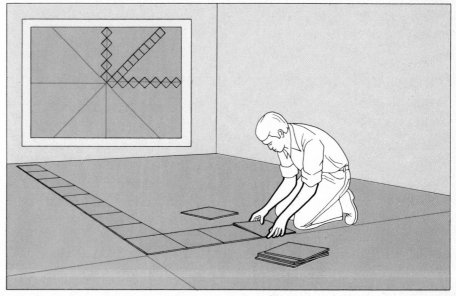

Setting the Tiles

Setting tiles and adhesive. With a notched trowel held at a 45° angle to the floor, spread adhesive along one chalk line—if you are laying tiles in an on-the-square pattern—working from the intersection toward a wall. Leave parts of the line uncovered for guidance, and make your layer about half the thickness of your tile. Set this row of tiles, butting each tile against one already laid and dropping it into place. Do not slide a tile: that will force adhesive onto its surface. Set another row of tiles along the perpendicular chalk line, then fill the area between the rows in a pyramid pattern so that each new tile butts against two already laid *(inset, top)*. When you finish a section, roll it with a rented 100-pound linoleum roller or a rolling pin on which you place most of your weight. To lay a diagonal pattern *(inset, bottom)*, set tiles point to point over the perpendicular chalk lines. Lay another row of tiles with their sides along the diagonal chalk line. Then fill in the area between rows, working from the intersection toward the wall.

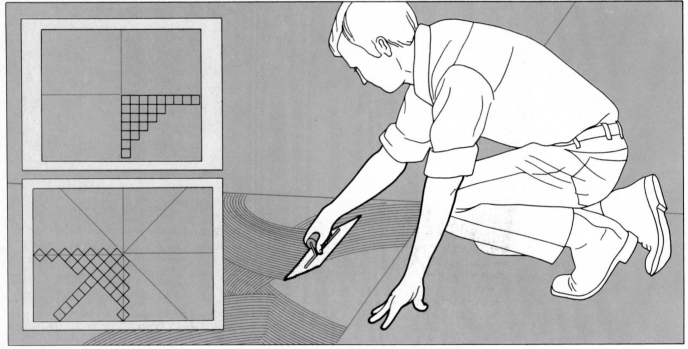

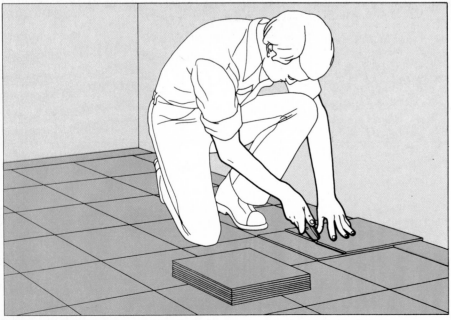

Trimming a border tile. Place two loose tiles squarely on top of the last whole tile in a row and slide the upper one across the untiled gap until it touches a wall; then, using the edge of the top tile as a guide, score the one beneath with a utility knife. Snap the tile along the scored line. The piece that was not covered by the guide tile will fit into the border, its snapped edge against the wall. Cut oddly shaped tiles—those around door moldings, for example—by the methods shown on pages 32-33.

If your floor is diagonally laid, score tiles from corner to corner, using a straightedge, and snap them to make triangular half tiles to fill the sawtooth edge of the diagonal pattern. If you also have a square-set border, trim tiles for it as above.

Two Patterns for Parquetry

Parquet—wood tile—comes in a variety of sizes and shapes with which you can lay a handsome floor in patterns such as the two traditional ones shown below, "Haddon Hall" and "Herringbone." Design and installation techniques are much like those for resilient tile floors, but there are a few exceptions. When you plot your design on graph paper (page 47), you may have to use more than one square of the graph to represent each tile, depending on the shape of tile you are using. And if you are using square tiles, indicate on the plot the direction of the grain in each tile. In elongated tiles, the grain runs lengthwise.

While resilient tile floors have a border of trimmed tile on four sides, wood floors should have a border of whole tiles on the sides of the room where there are doorways, because the glue under a full-sized wood tile provides a stronger bond in heavily trafficked areas. Guidelines are set up just as they are for resilient tile (page 47), but when you make a dry run, you may need to adjust the lines to get a full-tile border on a door side.

Wood tiles absorb moisture, so before you lay them let them rest loosely around the room for 72 hours so that they will adjust to the humidity. Also, leave a ½-inch space between the border tiles and the walls to allow for the tiles' expansion. Insert a thin strip of ½-inch cork, available at lumberyards, in the space.

Spread mastic for wood tiles ⅛ inch thick and allow to set for two hours, until it is tacky. Then lay the tiles, paying special attention to the grain patterns marked on your plot and to locking tongues and grooves tightly together.

Laying the "Herringbone" pattern. Lay the first 6-by-12-inch tile along a diagonal guideline, one corner set in the intersection. Lay the second tile at the end of and perpendicular to the first, and the third tile at the end of and perpendicular to the second, as shown. Use the chalk lines and these three tiles as guides for laying the next three and continue until you reach the wall. Repeat in the other sections of the room until you have completed the floor (inset).

Setting wood tiles in place. Making sure that the grain pattern duplicates that on your graph paper, slip a wood tile into position so its tongue and groove fit with those of adjacent tiles. Tap it with a mallet cushioned by a wood block while holding adjacent tiles in place. The tiles should be laid in the pyramidal manner used for resilient tiles (opposite, top). Measure border tiles as you would resilient tiles (opposite, bottom), but mark them with a pencil instead of scoring them, and cut them with a fine-toothed handsaw.

Laying the "Haddon Hall" pattern. Starting at the intersection of your guidelines, lay an 18-inch square of four 6-by-12-inch tiles bordering one 6-by-6-inch tile. The first two 6-by-12-inch tiles should be laid perpendicular to one another along the guidelines. Lay the floor pyramidally from this block until it is complete (inset).

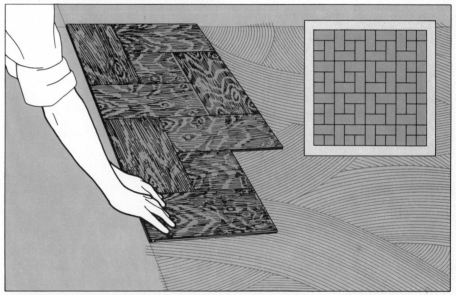

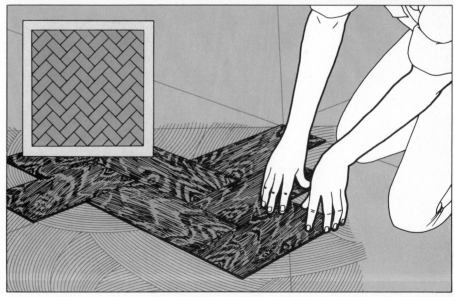

Template for a Cut-to-Fit Floor

Sheet vinyl provides the springiness and pattern variety of resilient tile in an essentially seamless surface—moisture-proof and dirt-resisting. In large rooms, vinyl is laid like cushion-back carpet *(pages 110-111);* the material is unrolled, trimmed to fit and fastened in place with adhesive. In small areas like the one shown on these pages, a floor pattern cut from 15-pound building felt can speed the job. The pattern is laid on the sheet vinyl and the flooring is cut to fit.

Guidelines must be scratched onto the felt and the sheet vinyl with a tool called a scriber, available at hardware stores. The scriber resembles a school compass fitted with a second sharp point in place of the pencil, and has a knurled nut that locks the points at any spacing you choose. To mark very resilient sheet vinyls, on which scratches may not show, replace one of the scriber points with a grease pencil or a felt-tipped pen.

Begin the job by removing any shoe moldings *(page 24)* and rough-cutting the felt to lie flat in the room. Then run one point of the scriber around the walls; the other point will scratch the outline of the room and all its interruptions onto the felt. Lay the vinyl out flat in another room for 24 hours to adjust to room temperature. Then spread the felt pattern over the sheet of vinyl and reverse the scribing procedure: run one point along the scratches on the felt; the other will mark the room's outline on the vinyl. Cut the vinyl out and lay it into the room.

Fold the sheet halfway back upon itself and, using a notched trowel, coat the floor with a nonflammable, water- or latex-based adhesive; use a type recommended for the material being applied *(page 28).* Roll the vinyl over the adhesive and repeat the procedure.

Because sheet vinyl comes in widths up to 15 feet, you may be able to avoid seams except for the short ones necessary to fit the vinyl around obstacles. At such places, slit the vinyl from its nearest edge, then make a cutout for the pipe or post. When you lay the flooring, repair the slits with a seam-sealing fluid, available from flooring dealers, which makes the joint almost invisible.

1 **Fitting the felt.** Unroll the felt, dark side up, along the longest side of the room, slicing with a utility knife about an inch from the walls, stairs, doorcasings and all permanent obstructions. Fasten one end of the strip to the floor with thumbtacks across its width. Then crawl from that end of the room to the other, running your hands over the felt ahead of you to stroke it smooth; insert tacks at about 2-foot intervals to hold the felt flat. Lay, trim and tack as many sheets as necessary to cover the room, overlapping them about 6 inches.

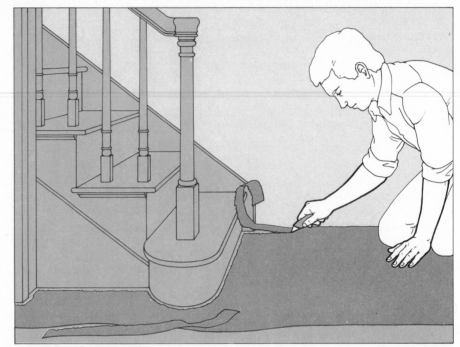

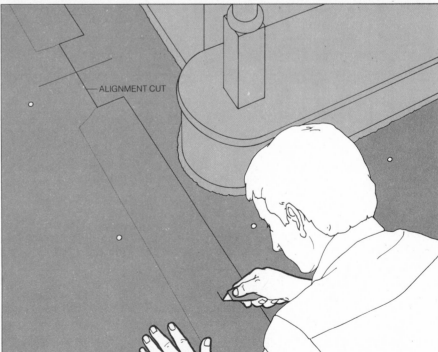

— ALIGNMENT CUT

2 **Cutting notches to align the sheets.** Every 2 feet along an overlap between sheets, make an 8-inch alignment cut through both sheets with a utility knife. Make additional cuts from the ends of the alignment cut to the edge of the top sheet and discard the rectangular scrap you have cut out. Reach under the notch and cut or tear away a similar notch along the edge of the bottom sheet. The sheets will butt along the alignment cut; the other cuts or tears are not critical. Chalk a short line across the alignment cut, marking both sheets.

3 **Scribing the pattern.** Set the points of a scriber about 2 inches apart and, keeping an imaginary line between the points perpendicular to the walls, doorcasings or stair risers, pull one point around the edge of the room, letting it ride along the walls; the other point will scratch a line onto the felt. The span between the points must not change during the job; to check the setting, scribe part of a circle onto the felt *(inset),* and periodically set the points at the center and rim of the circle.

Remove the thumbtacks and carry the felt to the room where you have unrolled the vinyl.

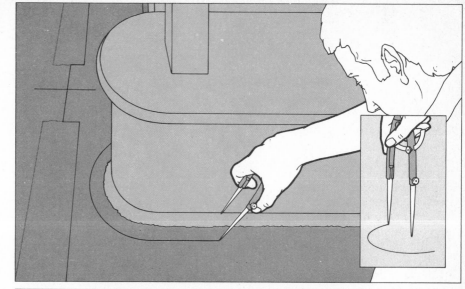

4 **Positioning the pattern.** Lay the sheets of felt on the vinyl, butting top and bottom sheets at each alignment notch and lining up the chalk marks across them. Slide the felt pattern over the vinyl so that any pattern in the vinyl will line up along the longest wall, using the scriber to check the final position. (Remember that you will cut the vinyl as far outside the scribed lines as the distance between the scriber points.) Thumbtack the pattern to the vinyl—the pinholes will not show after the vinyl is laid.

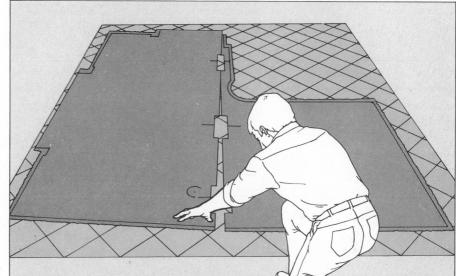

5 **Cutting the vinyl.** Holding the scriber exactly as you did in Step 3, trace the scribed line on the felt with one scriber point; the other point will scratch a cutting line on the surface of the vinyl. If a scratched line does not show up on the vinyl, replace one point of the scriber with a felt-tipped pen or a grease pencil, using the partial circle on the felt to check the setting. Cut through the flooring along the cutting lines with a utility knife; the common straight blade will serve, but many professionals prefer a hooked linoleum blade, available at hardware stores.

Lay the flooring into position in the room. Fold one side halfway back and spread adhesive onto the underlayment *(page 48)*. Set the flooring back into position and roll out any air bubbles with a heavy roller, borrowed from your flooring dealer, or with a rolling pin. Fold back the other side, spread adhesive and roll. Finally, replace all base shoe moldings and tack edging strips over exposed vinyl edges, as in doorways.

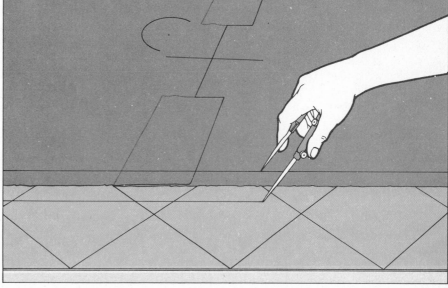

Embedding Stone and Ceramic Tiles in Mortar

For many floors, the merits of hard mineral materials may well outweigh the desirability of resilience provided by wood or vinyl. Vestibules, halls, hearths and bathrooms can benefit from the beauty and durability of tiles of ceramic or stone. While hard tiles are best laid in a thin bed of mortar over a concrete subfloor, as described on these pages, modern adhesives make it possible to lay them on underlayment of ⅝-inch exterior-grade plywood, using the methods for laying resilient tiles *(pages 46-48)*.

The hard surfacing materials come in a dazzling variety. Ceramic-tile retailers, supplied by artisans abroad as well as a big domestic industry, offer choices that range from unglazed earth-colored pavers 6 inches square and ¼ inch thick, and 8-inch square quarry tiles ½ inch thick, to colorful glazed and patterned creations up to a foot square. Use tiles with abrasive grain fired into the glaze if you want to reduce slipperiness.

Slate and various kinds of sandstone, limestone and quartzite, all available in tile-shaped rectangles of uniform thickness, also make good-looking, impermeable floors and can be laid like ceramic; however, irregularly shaped flagstones, widely used for vestibules, require a special method *(page 55)*.

But for millennia the most desirable of all stones has probably been lustrous, gemlike marble. Though marble tiles come in various dimensions, a common and practical size is 1 foot square—½ inch thick if American, 1 centimeter (²/₅ inch) thick if imported from Europe. Marble honed to a soft gloss is best for floors; highly polished surfaces are slippery and easily scratched. Despite its density, marble absorbs liquids, but transparent silicone sealer will protect it, and poultices *(page 35)* will clean most stains.

While the methods given here apply to a bare concrete subfloor, they can also be used to lay new ceramic or stone tiles in mortar over sound old tile floors; however, the floor level will rise about ⅝ inch. The original surface must be level to within ⅛ inch. By rolling a straight piece of pipe in various directions, find high and low spots. Level high spots with a rub brick or a rented concrete grinder, and fill low spots with mortar.

If your tiles have a directional pattern, such as the grain of marble, arrange a number of them to determine whether to set them with the grain running one way, or in a checkerboard-parquet style or at random. Lay out the tiles, using the method shown on page 47, but in place of chalk lines stretch mason's string tautly between nails driven into the wall plates ¾ inch from the floor.

The technique given here uses a thinset mortar, which can be made by mixing three cups of portland cement and three cups of fine masonry sand into two cups of latex tile-setting liquid (a bond-strengthening suspension of latex in water, sold by cement dealers). A batch will cover 6 square feet. It is applied with a rectangular "box-notch" trowel.

The job is finished, for most vestibules and halls, with wood baseboards and base shoes—the ones you removed, or new ones. For a formal look or for protection against splashes in bathrooms, make bases of the same material as the floor. Ceramic tilemakers can supply such trim. For stone floors, you can make your own base trim by sawing 12-by-12 tiles into 4-by-12 strips. Smooth and bevel or round the rough edges with silicon-carbide sanding disks in an electric drill, using grits 80, 150 and 320 in succession. Secure the trim to the wall with water-resistant organic adhesive.

1 **Making the mortar bed.** Dampen the concrete subfloor and, starting in one of the corners where the reference strings cross, use a box-notch trowel to spread a low mound of mortar. Then hold the trowel nearly vertical, and drag the teeth on the subfloor so you leave a row of mortar ridges. Do not try to substitute a saw-tooth-edged mastic trowel for this job; teeth ¼ inch deep and ¼ inch apart are necessary to get the mortar to the correct level.

2 **Laying the first tile.** Place a tile on the ridged mortar with one corner at the crossed strings, and while twisting it slightly several times press it down firmly; use full body weight on big tiles. With the handle of a mason's trowel, tap the edges of the tile until it lines up exactly with the strings. Check with a level along both dimensions and diagonally; tap down any high sides. Pick up any excess mortar for reuse.

It is wise to check your first tile by lifting it off the mortar to determine whether it made full contact; if it did not, then make a new bed with more mortar and re-lay the tile with more twisting and pressure. Dampen the backs of highly absorbent tiles with a sponge. If you are using quarry tiles that have deeply scored backs, trowel mortar into the scores before setting.

3 **Filling in the field.** Lay tiles, aligned with strings, in all four directions from the first; let the cross thus formed set overnight, remove the strings and then fill in the quarters. Unless the tiles have self-spacing lugs cast on their bottom edges, use rounded toothpicks to hold them ³⁄₃₂ inch apart. Since tiles may not be cut to precise size, measure frequently from the center lines and adjust spacing to keep joints squared. With a level on a straight 2-by-4, check and adjust the height of the tiles against the central tile as you set them. At obstacles, use the techniques shown on pages 32-33.

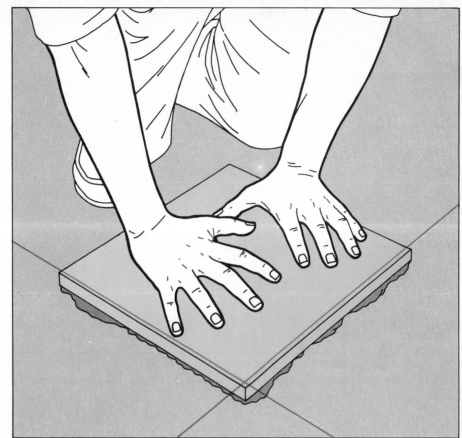

4 Cutting border tiles. Cut stone or thick ceramic tiles—marked to measure for the floor's border by the method shown on page 48—with a silicon-carbide masonry blade in a circular saw. Clamp the tile between a guide strip and a 2-by-10 on sawhorses; use wood scraps as thick as the tile to carry the saw at the beginning and end of the cut. Prepare for dust: work outdoors if possible, and wear goggles and a respirator. Make the cut in two passes, the first ¼ inch deep, the second with the blade set to extend below the tile ⅛ inch into the 2-by-10. Cut small, thin ceramic tiles with a rented tile cutter (*below, right*). Push the handle forward to draw the scoring wheel across the tile's surface; then flip the handle back and gently tap it, so that the flanges on both sides of the wheel will strike the tile and snap it along the scored line.

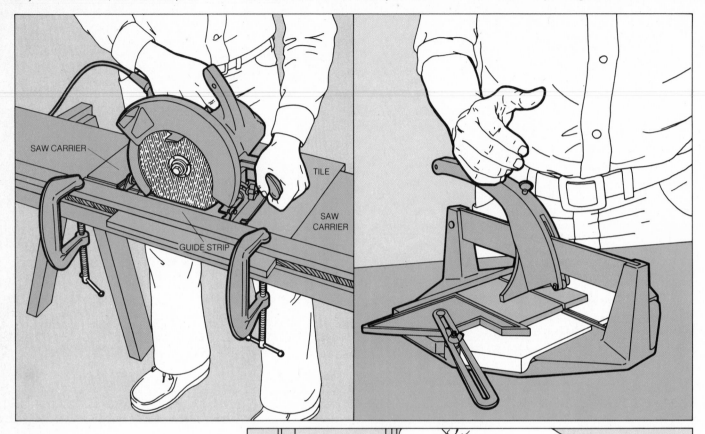

SAW CARRIER

TILE

SAW CARRIER

GUIDE STRIP

5 Setting a threshold. For ceramic or marble tile floors, a marble threshold is generally installed in interior doorways by removing the doorstops with a putty knife and pry bar, then setting the threshold in a bed of raked mortar as you would a tile (*right*). Saw off the doorstops to fit and replace them. Marble companies cut thresholds to length and bevel them to accommodate the newly tiled floor to its neighbors. Bathroom thresholds should rise ¼ inch above the floor to make a dam against spills. Outside doors may need new weatherproof metal thresholds.

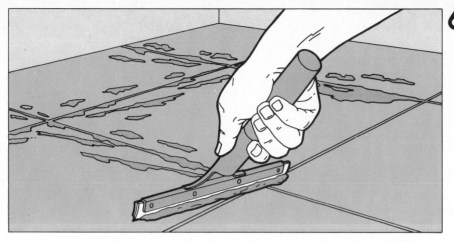

6
Grouting between tiles. Using a window-washing squeegee, pack into the spaces between tiles a grout of portland cement and latex tile-setting liquid mixed in proportions that make it barely fluid. Squeegee each joint from both directions, crossing the tile edges at a slight angle. Then use a damp cloth to wipe the tiles and recess the grout slightly. As soon as the grout starts to set, clean the film of cement from the tiles by sponging with water. The gray grout made with portland cement is inconspicuous and does not show dirt, but if you wish, add powdered coloring, available from building-supply dealers.

The Informal Charm of a Flagstone Floor

Flagstone's natural texture, color and jigsaw-puzzle jointing make it an intriguing material for both vestibules and hallways. Quarried from the sedimentary stones—limestone, sandstone, bluestone or slate—it comes in an array of sizes, shapes and colors, although thickness is generally between ¼ inch and ¾ inch. You can buy it or even find pieces of usable thickness at the base of a fragmenting cliff, ready-split and in interesting shapes. Whether you buy it or collect it, select the pieces with an eye to color; stones that seem similar when seen one at a time may appear too contrasty when set side by side.

Because flagstones will be somewhat uneven on both sides, they cannot be laid in the thin-set mortar used for tiles. Instead, plan to tamp them into a bed of mortar ¾ to 1¼ inches thick.

If you lay flagstones in mortar on a wood subfloor, double the joists (pages 16-17) to bear extra weight, and add plywood underlayment. Lay a 90-pound felt-paper base and ungalvanized 2 x 2 reinforcing mesh with 10-gauge wire to strengthen the mortar.

The esthetics of a flagstone floor depend mostly on layout, which should be planned in a dry run. Search for pieces with edges sufficiently straight to meet the walls at the border. Fill in by finding larger stones that join approximately with the borders and with one another, even if they leave some sizable gaps; then look for smaller flagstones to fill the gaps. Keep the joints to an inch or less, allowing occasional exceptions.

Some stones will need trimming. You can fit the softer kinds of stone, such as sandstone, by chipping with a bricklayer's hammer (or an old carpenter's hammer, since the hammer face may get marred). First, undercut the edge by chipping along its lower side (below), and then chip away the resulting sharp overhang. Cut harder stones by sawing a shallow score as you would marble (opposite page, Step 4), then tapping the score with a hammer and a stone chisel until the stone breaks in two.

Make mortar of one part portland cement, three parts masonry sand and just enough water so that a trowel stuck into the batch will not fall over. To ensure a tight bond between a concrete subfloor and the mortar, apply a latex or epoxy bonding agent, available from building-supply dealers, to the floor just before troweling on the mortar.

Lay down mortar for one stone, then brush the back of the stone with a cream-thick mixture of cement and water. Press the stone firmly in place and, with a rubber mallet, level it (page 53, Step 2). Make sure subsequent stones are roughly level with the first by using a level and a 2-by-4 (page 53, Step 3). Grout the joints with mortar, troweled in and recessed slightly by drawing a piece of pipe along the seam. Mist the floor with water and let it cure for three days under polyethylene sheeting.

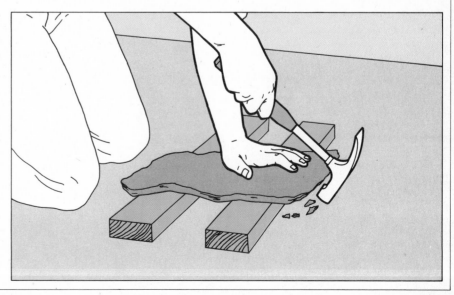

Pouring a Concrete Floor for a Basement

The dirt-floored basement found in many old homes lets in dampness and cold. Covering it with concrete not only cures those ills but completes the major part of the job of converting waste space into a usable room. Pouring the concrete is a relatively fast operation; preparing the layers of gravel, steel reinforcement and plastic that underlie the concrete slab and keep it dry will consume more time.

Before you start such a job, check the local building code. The minimum height specified is generally 7 feet 6 inches; to this height you must add 8 inches to allow for the slab and the layer of gravel beneath it. Since dirt-floored basements have lower ceilings than this, you probably will have to do some digging and disposing of dirt. In homes where the

foundation does not extend down at least 8 feet 2 inches from the joists, you will need professional help to reinforce the foundation. You may also have to provide special platforms to hold the furnace and hot-water heater—they should rest above the new floor level.

Before you begin digging, set up guidelines for a drainage grade. The floor should slant down to one corner of the room where if you fear serious water problems you will install a liner for a sump pump, an electrically powered automatic device that begins working whenever the water level underneath the slab rises. Besides grading the floor, you will need to dig channels for drain tiles *(Step 4)*, perforated plastic tubes that distribute water through the gravel.

The easiest way to pour is all at once. A transit-mix company will provide the concrete and deliver it to your house, sending it into the basement through a chute in a window. However, a truck loaded with enough concrete for the average basement floor weighs 26 to 30 tons and can damage lawns, driveways and septic systems. It may be simpler to divide the floor with wood frames and pour in sections *(page 58)*, getting concrete in smaller batches. Some ready-mix is delivered in small trucks, or you can haul it yourself in a rented trailer or even move the concrete from street to basement in wheelbarrows. The last option requires several strong helpers—a wheelbarrow loaded with concrete weighs 300 pounds—and a convoy of wheelbarrows.

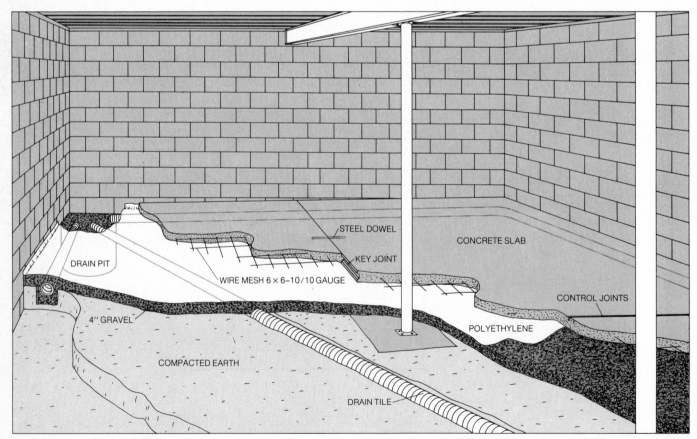

The anatomy of a basement floor. The bottom layer is tightly compacted dirt, graded down toward one corner of the room. Drain tiles run to the low corner, where a pit filled with gravel absorbs all the excess water. If you fear a serious water problem, install a sump pump in this corner to ensure against any flooding. On top of the dirt is a 4-inch layer of gravel, which provides drainage and a firm base for the concrete. It is topped by moisture-blocking polyethylene sheeting. Then wire mesh reinforcement is centered in the concrete *(page 60)* and control joints, which allow for expansion, are cut into the slab at 10-foot intervals *(page 61)*. In the basement shown here, the concrete was poured in two different sections; they are locked together by key joints and steel bars *(pages 58-59)* so that they will not spread apart or sink.

Laying the Groundwork

1 **Establishing the drainage grade.** After digging away the old dirt floor so that it is approximately 8 inches below the level desired for the new floor, cut a 2-by-4 to the planned ceiling height and hold it against the wall in a corner, one end resting against a floor joist. Mark the floor line on the wall at the bottom of the 2-by-4 with a nail. Repeat in the other corner. In one corner—use the one planned for a sump pump if you need it—mark the lowest point of the floor. It should be sloped 1 inch in every 8 feet from the floor-line mark on the other corner of that wall.

2 **Marking the grade.** Snap chalk lines between the floor-line mark and the nails in the corners of adjoining walls. Then snap chalk lines between the nails on the other two walls. Drive nails into the walls every 4 feet along the chalk lines that run the length of the room. Then drive nails into the midpoints of the chalk lines that run the width of the room.

3 **Grading the floor.** Tie lengths of string tautly across the room between the nails set in the lengthwise walls. Then divide the room in half by tying string between the nails set at the midpoints of the shorter pair of walls. If there is a post in the middle of the room, tie the dividing string to it. With a pick and shovel, grade the floor so it is 8 inches below the strings at all points.

In the lowest corner of the room dig a hole 24 inches wide and 28 inches deep and, unless you are installing a sump pump, fill it with 1-inch clean gravel. Starting at the hole, dig a trench 4 inches deep, 6 inches wide and 4 inches from the walls all around the room. Then dig a trench of the same dimensions from the hole diagonally across the room. Clear away the dirt and put a 2-inch layer of gravel into the trenches.

4 **Installing drain tile.** Lay drain tile on the gravel in the trenches so that it forms a continuous conduit around the room and another along the diagonal trench, both running into the hole. If you are installing a sump pump, cut out the drain-tile holes marked on the sump pump liner, insert the ends of the tubes and set the liner in the hole.

Tamp loose dirt firmly down using a 1-foot square of plywood with a 2-by-4 nailed to it for a handle or a rented, gas-powered tamper. Restring knocked-down lines and recheck to make sure the floor is 8 inches below the grading guidelines.

Getting Ready for the Pour

1 Making key-jointed form boards. Plane a ¼-inch bevel on the edges of one face of 1-by-2s to make key-joint molds for as many form boards as you need. Snap chalk lines along the faces of 2-by-4s, 1 inch from each edge. Nail the 1-by-2 key-joint molds between the chalk lines, beveled edges out, with eightpenny finishing nails.

Make enough lengths of form with key-joint molds to span the room's length plus enough extra ones to span half the width: if the pouring and spreading of the concrete is interrupted, set the extra forms up to make a smaller slab. After it has set, pour the rest of the floor; the key joint then will lock the slabs together (*inset*).

2 Constructing the forms. Lay a key-jointed form board (*Step 1*) across two 2-by-4s and drill ¾-inch holes for steel bars through each key joint and form board—one hole in the center of each form and one a foot from each end. Nail three 1-by-2 stakes 16 inches long to the back of each form board, aligning the tops of the stakes with the upper edge of the form board.

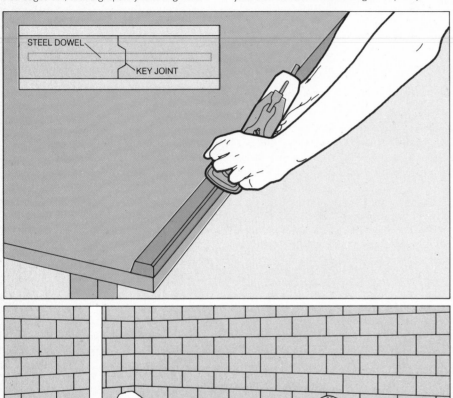

STEEL DOWEL

KEY JOINT

3 Setting up the forms. Line the forms up along the guideline that divides the basement so that the key-joint molds face the side of the room you will pour first. Have a helper hold one end of each form in place while you drive the stakes into the ground until the top of the form is aligned with the string. Check the grade with a level.

4 Bracing the forms. Drive 18-inch bracing stakes that are made from 1-by-2s into the dirt behind the forms, angling them to the top of the forms, and nail the stakes and forms together. Splice the forms where they meet by nailing 1-by-2s across the joints. Then make sure all forms are perfectly upright.

Drive a row of steel reinforcing bars into the dirt halfway between the forms and the wall. You should make sure that the top of each bar is level with the guidelines.

5 Laying the gravel. Spread a 4-inch layer of gravel over the dirt, checking to be sure the gravel is 4 inches below the lines at every point. You will need 1½ tons of gravel per 80 square feet.

Remove the guidelines and spread sheets of 4-mil polyethylene over the gravel, overlapping the sheets 18 inches. To prevent the slab from bonding to the basement walls—it must be free to shift—prop the edges of the plastic against the walls up to the chalk lines.

6 Reinforcing with steel. Lay reinforcing wire mesh—the type called 6x6-10/10 gauge—over the gravel, overlapping the pieces and twisting their edges together. The outside edges of the mesh should be 1 inch from forms and walls.

Insert smooth steel dowels 18 inches long and ½ inch in diameter through the holes in the form boards so that half the exposed length of a bar is on either side of the form. Insert wood wedges in the holes from the back of the form to lock the dowels in place while you pour the concrete.

REINFORCING BAR

7 Reinforcing the forms. Shovel gravel against the back of the forms to help hold them upright and to prevent concrete from seeping under the forms while you are pouring. Then tie asphalt-impregnated isolation joints around any basement posts. Finally, coat the forms and the steel dowels with grease to prevent the concrete from bonding to them.

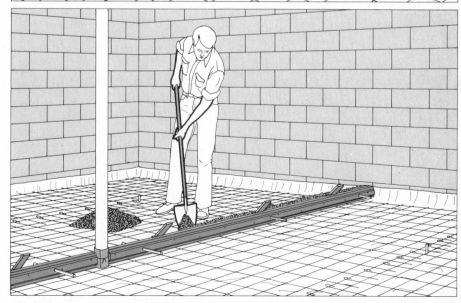

Spreading Concrete to Make a Smooth and Level Slab

If you have ordered ready-mix concrete, be prepared for the truck. You will have to spread the concrete before it sets, and pay overtime charges if the truck waits over 45 minutes. If your local code requires an inspection of the site before pouring, have it done before the truck arrives. Complete the preparations that are described below, and have helpers equipped with protective gloves and boots waiting for the truck.

If the concrete is being delivered by truck, the most efficient way to get it into your basement is by using a chute. Most transit-mix dealers provide 10 feet of chute, so the truck may have to drive onto your property to get near enough. Lay a path of 2-by-10 planks to protect your lawn and driveway. Cover all exterior walls around the basement window and the ground under it with polyethylene sheeting to catch spilled concrete.

When you order the concrete, tell the dealer how much you need—a 4-inch slab needs 1 cubic yard of concrete per 80 square feet of floor—and specify its consistency. Consistency is measured by "slump," the number of inches a cone-shaped mass of concrete, 8 inches high, will decrease in height, or slump, when the conical form is lifted off. Generally you need a 4-inch slump, 5 inches if you are transporting the concrete from the street in wheelbarrows.

The pouring and spreading of the concrete must go quickly (below). Fill each section before you move to the next—the aggregate will break down, weakening the floor, if the wet concrete is shifted too often. As soon as the forms are filled, remove the excess concrete with a screed (Step 2) and use a darby (Step 3) to tamp down the aggregate that rises to the top of the slab.

Once the form is filled, the work goes more slowly. Wait 15 minutes to four hours for bleed water to disappear before you can proceed to the final finishing step, troweling. To speed the job, you may wish to use a power troweler as shown on page 63, Step 4.

After troweling, the slab must cure—the chemicals in the concrete interact with water, giving strength to the floor. You can use a curing compound, available from building suppliers, for this process, or take steps to keep the floor damp for at least one week.

1 Spreading the concrete. As the concrete slides down the chute from a ready-mix truck, have helpers transfer it to the forms in wheelbarrows. Spread the concrete with a hoe and a shovel. When you have filled up a section, pull the reinforcing wire halfway up the thickness of the wet concrete slab with a rake. Check frequently to see that the steel dowels remain in place and the forms are upright.

2 **Leveling the surface.** With a screed made by nailing two 2-by-4s to a third, level a section along the center of the slab to the top of the reinforcing bars. Drive the bars below the surface with a 2-pound sledge hammer, then work the surface on either side of the path until it is level with the top of the form and the nails in the walls. Have a helper stand by to take off excess, and shovel more concrete into low spots in the surface.

3 **Floating the surface.** As soon as the surface is level, smooth the concrete with a rented darby—a board about 4 inches wide and 6 feet long with a handle. "Bleed" water will rise to the surface. When it disappears and the shiny surface becomes dull, cut the control joints and finish (*Steps 4 and 5*). To be sure that the concrete is ready, throw a 1-inch stone onto it; the stone should bounce, leaving only a small indentation.

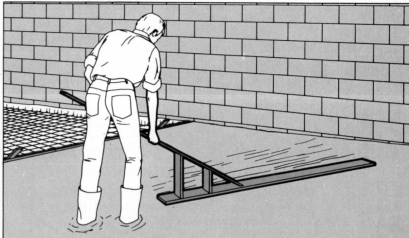

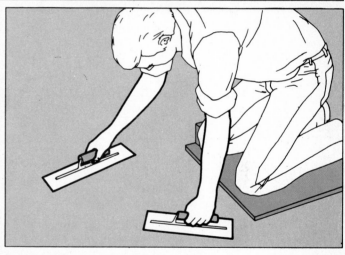

4 **Cutting control joints.** Have a helper kneel on 2-by-10 boards laid across the concrete while he cuts control joints every 10 feet, running the jointing tool along the board edges and pressing firmly to make grooves 1 inch deep.

5 **Finishing.** While your helper cuts control joints, kneel on kneeboards—sheets of ¾-inch plywood 2 feet square with a 2-by-4 block nailed to them for a handle—to smooth the surface with an aluminum float and a steel trowel. Lean on the trowel as you sweep the float in wide arcs across the concrete, then shift your weight to the float and use the trowel to smooth the marks you made. Move backward as you work until you have smoothed the entire surface; then trowel the slab a final time. You may have to dampen the concrete to keep it workable.

When the concrete is dry enough to walk on (in about six hours), sprinkle it lightly with water and cover it with polyethylene sheeting. After the concrete has cured for 24 hours, remove the forms and pour the second slab.

Resurfacing a Concrete Floor

When a concrete floor is so badly cracked and pitted that repairs are impractical, the solution is a new surface made by pouring a ¾- to 2-inch layer of concrete over the old slab. By the same method you can install a concrete slab over a wood subfloor to provide a base on which to lay tiles *(pages 52-55).*

Only structurally sound floors can be resurfaced. Concrete floors that have buckled or heaved because of inadequate drainage or improperly compacted subsoil should be replaced. Sags in a wood subfloor should be repaired and the joists should be reinforced before resurfacing *(pages 14-23).*

Since the resurfacing layer is thin, you can mix concrete for it by hand *(page 34)* if the area is less than 80 square feet. For an area between 80 and 160 square feet, rent a power mixer; for areas larger than that, rent a 1-cubic-yard, haul-it-yourself container to transport concrete from a transit-mix company to your house. One cubic yard of concrete is enough for a 320-square-foot slab 1 inch thick.

If your concrete surface is to be laid over a wood subfloor, prepare the floor by tacking down a layer of 15-pound asphalt felt and covering it with ungalvanized 2 × 2-10/10 wire mesh. This reinforces the cement and protects it from movement in the subfloor. If you are resurfacing a concrete slab, etch the floor with acid *(right, above)* to provide a bonding surface. Just before you pour the new slab, coat the old one with a bonding slurry of 1 part portland cement, 1 part sand and ½ part latex. The resurfacing concrete is made of 1 part portland cement, 1 part sand and 1½ to 2 parts pea gravel. Do not use more than 5 gallons of water for each bag of cement.

For a large floor you may wish to make forms *(Step 2)* and pour the surface in sections. So that the new slab moves with the old, align the form boards over expansion joints. After pouring, control joints *(page 61, Step 4)* should be cut directly over those in the old slab.

A convenient finishing tool for a large floor is a rented gasoline-powered troweler; for smaller areas use the method described on page 61.

1 **Etching a concrete surface.** Using a heavy-bristled broom, brush a 27.9 per cent solution of muriatic acid onto the dampened concrete slab, using a gallon per 60 square feet of floor. Prepare the floor for the acid by removing loose concrete with a wire brush and washing the floor with a strong detergent. When the acid stops foaming, the etching is done; this takes only a few minutes. Neutralize the acid by washing the floor with household ammonia. Caution: when working with the acid, open windows for ventilation; wear goggles, rubber gloves and boots; and cover any exposed skin with petroleum jelly.

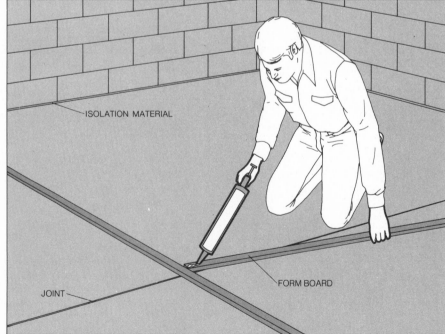

ISOLATION MATERIAL

JOINT

FORM BOARD

2 **Setting up the forms.** When pouring the floor in small sections, use a caulking gun to apply paneling adhesive to form boards the thickness of the resurfacing layer and stick them onto the slab. The adhesive will yield easily when you pull up the forms. Set the forms over expansion joints so the resurfacing concrete does not flow into them. Cut strips of asphalt-impregnated isolation material, which prevents the new concrete from bonding to the wall, and nail them to the walls. To provide guides for duplicating the joints on the new surface, mark the places where control joints on the old slab meet the forms or the walls.

3 **Bonding the new surface.** Dampen the section of the slab you are going to cover first and brush on the bonding slurry with a heavy-bristled broom. As soon as you coat the section, have a helper shovel or pour concrete into it. Use the form boards and isolation joints as guides for striking the excess concrete off the surface, then float the surface *(page 61)* to make it smooth and level. When the bleed water disappears, cut control joints through the new concrete down to the control joints in the old slab, using the marks on the form boards and walls as guides.

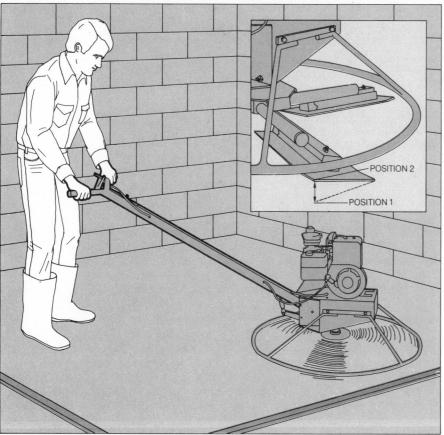

POSITION 2

POSITION 1

4 **Power troweling the surface.** When the concrete is still damp but hard enough to walk on, smooth it with a power troweler, its blades adjusted so they are flat against the surface *(inset, position 1)*. Move backward, pulling the machine. Have a helper hand-trowel *(page 61)* areas that you are unable to reach, sprinkling the surface with water if necessary to keep it workable. After troweling the entire surface, change the angle of the blades so that their leading edges are about an inch off the floor *(inset, position 2)*, and go over the concrete again, polishing it to a hard, glossy finish.

Pull up the form boards, replace them with asphalt-impregnated isolation joints, begin curing and pour the next section. After pouring the entire floor, let it cure for seven days.

Floors and Stairs as Art

In many houses, you can't see the floors for the furniture, or the chandeliers, or the pictures on the wall. Similarly ignored are the stairways. They often seem as if they were designed to be self-effacing—to be trodden and not viewed.

But in more and more new and renovated houses, the floors and stairways are key elements that help to establish the character of the whole house. They please the eye while they please the foot, and they help to define space.

The heightened emphasis on floors and stairways is a natural consequence of the 20th Century trend toward opening up compartmented living rooms into fluid, integrated spaces, while at the same time clearing them of all but the most basic—often built-in—furniture. As the walls have come down and the furniture has diminished, the floors and stairs have become increasingly prominent.

Designers are combining age-old materials and ideas with modern techniques to give floors conspicuous, unconventional and exciting surfaces. Clear polyurethane, applied with a brush or roller, now protects vulnerable painted floors—in and out of vogue since the time of the ancient Egyptians—from abrasive foot traffic. This same remarkable varnish has made covering floors with glued-down paper or printed fabric a realistic and increasingly popular option.

Rich-looking wood parquet obviously meets the demand for beauty in a floor that will be looked at, and comes in patterned, easily laid blocks like tiles. The intriguing possibilities for combining color, texture and design in ceramic tile are being increasingly exploited, helped by a world-wide surge in production and variety. And surfaces of stone and terrazzo gain an artful back-to-nature appeal when left rough and unpolished.

In large, open-plan interiors, flooring sometimes helps separate areas with different functions. Contrasting textures and colors visually segregate spaces that in many houses are no longer divided by physical barriers. Conversely, in an open plan that is broken into several levels, flooring in a single color or pattern can unify the various parts. In homes with minimal furnishing, carpet-covered platforms can serve as casual seating.

Stairways, possessed of the striking curves and angles that have enhanced the entry halls and stair wells of many great mansions, reveal heightened potentialities in opened-up interiors. The strong diagonal or spiral line of a balustrade, introduced into undefined and flowing space, makes an arresting focal point. Architects and designers in many modern homes treat stairways quite candidly as massive pieces of sculpture, structures that perform their pedestrian duty but also stand on their own as striking works of art.

Checks and balances. The spiral staircase in this Manhattan apartment is the dramatic focal point of a tiled entrance hall. The brown-and-beige carpet introduces a warm note of color into the all-white scheme. Its regular pattern visually interrupts the steep curve of the stair, helping to eliminate the feeling of vertigo sometimes communicated by spiral steps.

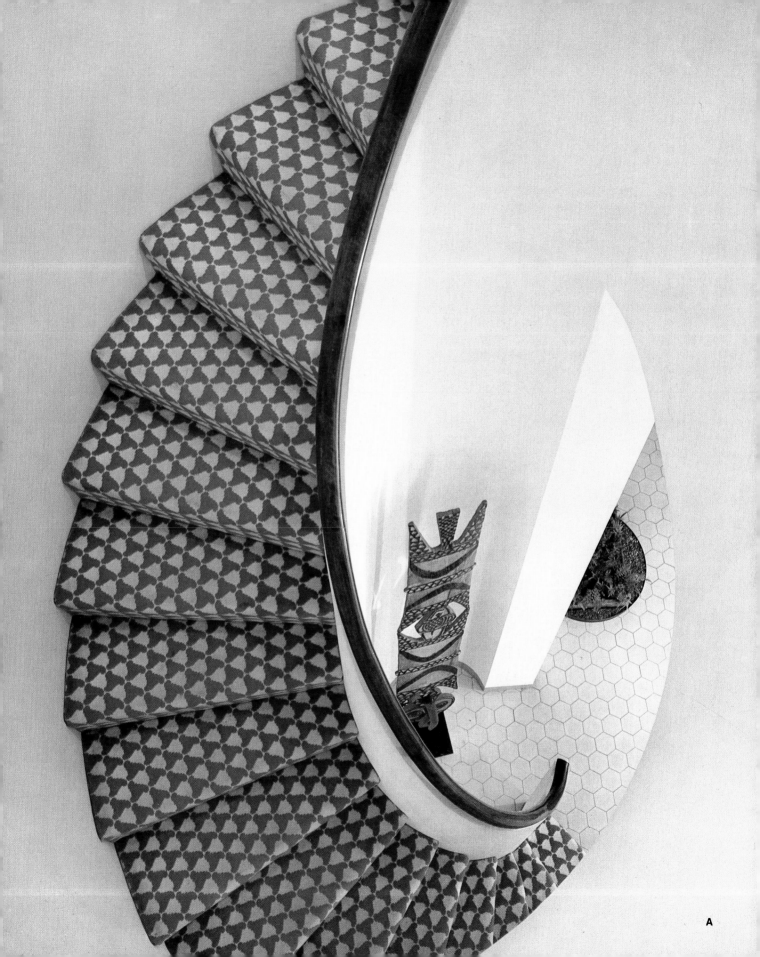

Rooms with an Inside View

Each of these three rooms could be stripped of its furnishings and each would still be a pleasure to look at. In all three, the floors make the rooms. The bold tiles in the picture at the right stand out from a deliberately bare interior. The imaginative rooms on the opposite page make use of techniques that are seldom employed on floors, to achieve startling decorative effects.

In one room, a French architect embeds small stones in concrete somewhat as stone chips are cemented in terrazzo—and then purposefully omits the machine polishing that flattens a terrazzo floor. The result is a nubbled, natural texture. In the other, a fool-the-eye "rug," which was designed and painted by the owner of the house, is an easily accomplished reflection of personal taste.

Eye-catching tiles. By neutralizing the other decor and selecting strongly colored tiles, the designer of this vacation house in northern Italy turns the eye downward with an old Mediterranean style. The anonymous white walls stand modestly aside to give the floor to the floor, a jewel case of handmade Tuscan tiles.

Out of the river and into the house. Small pebbles *(below)*, worn smooth in a riverbed, cover the floors of this home in Bordeaux. A mixture of cement, sand, water and stones was poured 2 inches thick onto a concrete base and flattened. As the mixture set, workmen washed away enough cement and sand to reveal the tops of pebbles near the surface and let the floor cure to bond them. In use, the traffic of shoe leather continually polishes the pebbles.

Painting a rug. Stenciled poppies cover old pine floorboards with a patterned, one-of-a-kind ''rug'' in the library of a renovated 19th Century Brooklyn townhouse. Ordinary paints—flat latex for the base and acrylic for the stencils—are protected by two coats of polyurethane varnish.

Carpets That Break the Rules

The conventional ways of using carpeting are not always the most attractive ways. Sisal matting, associated with casual residential interiors, makes a handsome covering for an office *(below)*. Conversely, carpeting that is designed for an office turns out to be equally at home in a home *(opposite, bottom)*.

In the form of rugs, carpeting has been used for centuries to set off an area from a background of flooring. In the apartment shown at the top of the opposite page, the arrangement is reversed: carpeting defines the dining area by surrounding it, and the bare tile floor becomes the room's focal point.

Over-the-wall carpeting. Sisal matting covers both the floor and the walls in the New York conference room of a shipping firm, giving the compact space a clean look and a nautical touch. The matting also deadens sound, which would make it as practical for a home recreation room as for this sleek office.

Carpet that divides. Flowing spaces, carpeted in lush red, encourage a casual style of life in this Milan apartment—and when the functions of the space change, so does the flooring material. No walls are needed to define this kitchen-dining area, tiled in black and white, as the ''room'' where the family takes its meals.

Carpet that unites. In this Fire Island vacation house, the living and dining areas are on separate levels. Carpeting covers the floors and steps and is carried over the built-in seating well and up the base of the half-sunken table—diners sit on the floor with their feet in the well—to unify all of the elements of the split-level space.

Stairs Made to Stare At

Through the ages, builders of monumental structures have been fascinated by the sculptural and decorative possibilities of stairs. Twenty-five centuries ago the Persian emperor Darius constructed twin reversing staircases, of 111 steps each, that still awe visitors to Persepolis. The heavily decorated spiral stairs in medieval Gothic cathedrals were designed to spin inspirationally heavenward.

Later, in England, imposing staircases added glamor to mansions and conferred status on their owners. Middle-class 19th Century Londoners built their homes around elaborate staircases such as the one below, to imitate the grand stairways in the country homes of the upper class.

These old forms have taken new shape in the hands of modern designers. Winding stairs, such as the one at right, have opened the traditional tight spiral corkscrew into smooth contemporary lines. And stark new shapes (*opposite*) recall, in poured concrete, the massive strength of ancient stone.

Sinuous showpiece. A daring curving staircase stands out boldly in a house full of French and English antiques. Part of a dramatic renovation that opened this narrow Manhattan townhouse into clean, modern spaces, the steel-frame stair whips upward from the basement to the top floor in four flights. At the dining-room level, its strong shape complements the curves of the traditional furniture—and masks an uninspiring view of the front door and entryway.

Victorian swoop. The showy staircase in this late-Victorian London townhouse is typical of hundreds built then. Ornate iron balusters support a railing designed to round corners and swoop upward without breaks for the customary corner newel posts and railing goosenecks.

Solid geometry. Massive, freestanding steps of reinforced concrete are a focal point of this contemporary villa near Milan, the rooms of which are a series of intersecting prisms. The concrete stairs were poured and cured outside the villa, then set into concrete footings that lie beneath the stainless-steel floor. The gleaming tubular steel railing and the spherical fireplace's metal chimney lead the eye up to the sharp planes of the angled ceiling.

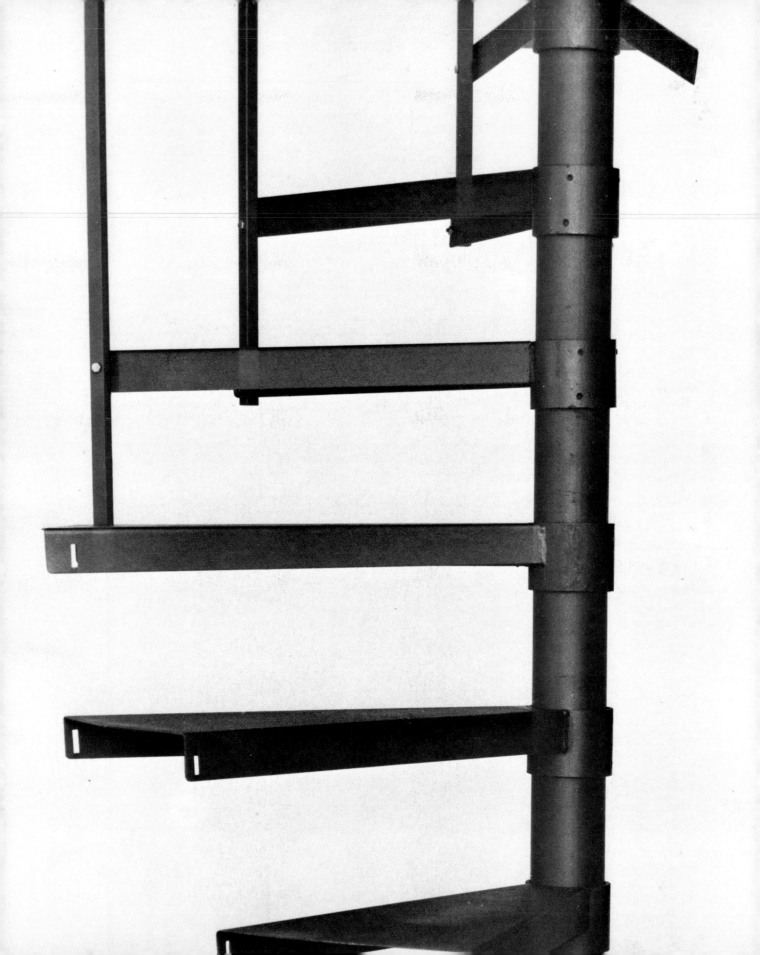

3

The Craftsmanship of Stairways

An iron spiral. This stark, compact stairway comes in a kit. To assemble it, the owner slides the treads to the bottom of a center pole, then raises them one by one to their permanent positions. Setscrews fasten the treads to the pole, and balusters, bolted to the front of each tread and the back of the one below it, establish the spiral and space the treads.

"To make a compleate *Stair-case,* is a curious peece of *Architecture,*" wrote the English architect Sir Henry Wotten in 1624. He went on to give stair builders some sage counsel on safety and comfort, recommending that a stairway "have a very liberall *Light,* against all casualtie of *Slippes,* and *Falles,*" advising that headroom should "bee large and *Airy*...because a man doth spend much breath in mounting," and stressing the merits of wide treads and an easy slope, "for our *Legges* doe labour more in *Elevation,* then in *Distension.*"

Sir Henry's concerns are shared by modern designers—with good reason. More accidents happen on stairways than in bathtubs. By far the leading causes of stairway accidents are tread defects, steepness and missing handrails. Therefore the safety problems of maintaining stairways *(pages 66-75)* and building them *(pages 76-93)* center on the treads, the degree of climb and the railing.

A slippery tread is a dangerous tread. To increase tread friction, avoid waxing bare wood; instead, cover the wood with abrasive paint or carpet. If infirm persons use a stairway, rubber treads may be advisable. A second tread defect is inadequate depth. In walking downstairs, most adults let their toes overhang the rounded nosing at the front of the tread. If a tread is 11¼ inches or more deep, the overhang is slight and the tread safe; but every reduction in depth raises the danger that a toe will slip over the nosing. In a well-designed staircase, each tread protrudes over the one below by about an inch, gaining tread depth without increasing the horizontal run.

The steepness of a stairway should not exceed 35°; at that angle there is relatively little danger that a person coming downstairs will pitch over. With a tread 11¼ inches deep and overhanging the one below it by 1¼ inches, a rise of 7 inches from one tread to the next creates the right slope. Moreover, each step should have exactly the same rise; uneven heights may be a factor in three fourths of all stairway accidents. Missing railings cause accidents, and the railings in place must be safe. This again is mostly a matter of dimensions. A handrail should stand 30 to 34 inches above the tread nosings and should be narrow enough—2⅝ inches at most—to be grasped firmly. A balustrade should be strong enough to take the weight of a falling adult. Safety experts recommend spacing balusters close enough so that a 5-inch sphere will not pass between them (the sphere they have in mind is a young child's head).

Lesser design dangers must also be guarded against: stairways too narrow for two persons to pass, doors that open over treads rather than over landings, improper lighting. And no stairway should run for more than 16 steps without a landing, an amenity that is essential, as architect Wotten put it, for "reposing on the way."

Intricate Structures, Simple to Repair

The structure of a stairway goes beyond that of hammer-and-saw carpentry to the stronger and more elegant techniques of cabinetwork, with its generous use of finish hardwood and ingenious joinery. For this reason a properly built stairway is not likely to present major problems. If it sags or bounces or seems unsafe, the cause is probably settling of the floor under the newel post or at the landing, which throws the stairway out of plumb and level and skews its right-angle joints. Jacking up the floor *(pages 14-23)* may restore the stairway's health, but if the damage is extensive (or if you judge that the original craftsmanship was poor), it may be wise to install a new prefabricated stairway *(pages 88-95)*.

But the commonest problems are relatively manageable ones such as squeaks, broken parts, a wobbly newel post or worn treads. The following pages offer an assortment of solutions. For many of these repairs you need to know how your stairway was built. Rough stairways, such as outside stairs or basement stairs *(pages 84-87)* are sometimes made by simpler methods, and metal spiral stairs *(pages 81-83)* are a special case, but among finished interior stairways made of wood there are only two basic types, defined by the way the treads are supported.

In most old stairways *(below)*, and sometimes in new ones built for special cases, thick sawtooth-notched boards called carriages support the treads and provide surfaces for nailing the risers, the vertical boards between treads. On a closed side—against a wall—a baseboard called a skirt-stringer, carefully sawed to fit against the treads and risers, covers and hides their ends. In the modern prefabricated stairway *(opposite, top)*, the functions of the carriage and the skirt-stringer are combined in one board, the housed stringer, grooved ½ inch deep to receive the ends of the treads and risers.

To discover which type of stairway you have, inspect the underside. In case the underside is enclosed behind walls, push a thin knife under the stringer at a tread end; if the knife is stopped by wood at a depth of ½ inch, the stairway has a housed stringer. If this test seems inconclusive, you will have to break a peephole through the enclosing wall.

Either kind of stairway may be open to the stair hall on one side or both. In such cases the visible trim is usually an open stringer cut to fit under the protruding tread ends and against the riser ends. In carriage stairways, it hides the rough wood of the carriage. In prefabricated stairways, the open stringer is cosmetic and structural: the treads rest on it and the risers are nailed to it.

Except for runs of four steps or less, open-sided stairways require a post-and-railing fence—an angled balustrade—to provide a handhold. The pickets, or balusters, are jointed into the railing and, usually, into the ends of the treads.

Two precautions are in order when repairing finished-wood stairways. Treads, risers, balusters, newel posts, railings and moldings are all made of hardwood—usually oak, birch, poplar or beech—and will split unless pilot holes are bored for all nails and screws. Secondly, glue, often used to repair treads and balusters, will not bond to dried glue; old joints must be scraped before they can be reassembled. Glue can also mar the finish of any wood it drips onto. Use it sparingly; if it runs, wipe it away immediately with a damp cloth, let the area dry and sand it.

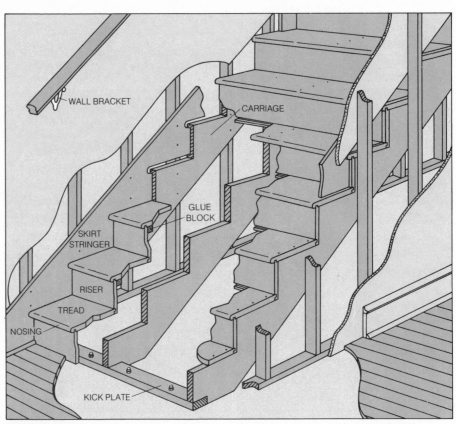

A carriage-supported stairway. In this stairway, which is constructed on the job at the same time that the house goes up, three 2-by-12 carriages with cutouts for each step run between floors, the two at the sides being spiked to the wall studs. At the bottom the carriages fit over a kick plate, a 2-by-4 nailed to the floor to keep them from sliding. After the ¾-inch risers are nailed to the carriages, the 1¹⁄₁₆-inch treads are pushed into place so that their back-edge tongues fit into the risers' grooves. At the same time a groove under the front edge of the tread drops over a tongue on the riser below. The tread is then nailed to the carriages. Each tread projects beyond the riser beneath it—usually by 1¼ inches—and ends in a rounded edge called a nosing. Glue blocks are used to reinforce the joints between the treads and risers at the front, and nails through the back riser into the tread strengthen that joint. The skirt-stringer that covers the tread and riser ends (and also hides nailheads there) is a ¾-inch piece of finish softwood, scribed and cut to fit perfectly. Wall brackets support handrails on each side.

A prefabricated stairway. Cut and assembled—minus the balustrade—in a mill, the stairway now used by most builders employs glue wedges to clamp the ends of the treads and risers in V-shaped notches, which are routed into the side of the housed stringer. The treads and risers usually meet in rabbet joints and are glue-blocked and nailed. A walled stairway would use housed stringers on both sides, but an open-sided stairway like this supports the outer ends of the treads on an open stringer cut like a carriage. Since it is too light to serve as a true carriage, the studding of the wall beneath it must be used to provide extra support.

The vertical cuts on the open stringer are mitered to match a miter at the end of the riser, thus concealing the end grain. The end of each tread has a return nosing nailed on, also hiding end grain. A return molding at the end and a scotia molding at the front complete the tread trim.

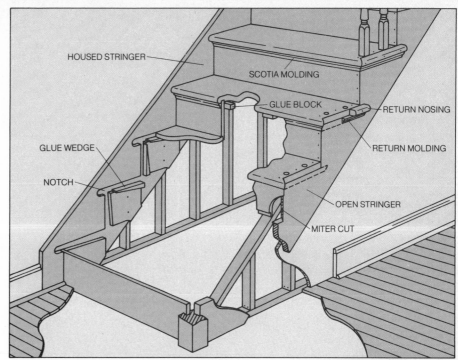

HOUSED STRINGER

SCOTIA MOLDING

GLUE BLOCK

RETURN NOSING

RETURN MOLDING

GLUE WEDGE

NOTCH

OPEN STRINGER

MITER CUT

The parts of a balustrade. Structural support for the railing comes from strong newel posts at the bottom and the landing. At its base the starting newel has slots called mortises to receive the ends of the first riser and the open stringer, and the newel sometimes extends through the floor to be bolted to a joist. Landing newels, similarly mortised, are bolted to the header joists (*page 92*) behind them. The railing is joined to the newels with rail bolts (*inset*). The lag-bolt end is screwed into the newel post, and the machine-screw end runs into a shank hole in the end of the railing. A washer and a nut are attached to the machine screw through an access hole bored from underneath the rail. The nut is tightened by driving a nail set against the notches in the nut. Then the access hole is plugged.

The railing rises to the upper newel in a curved piece called a gooseneck. Vertical balusters are installed between treads and the railing, usually with dowels but sometimes at the bottom with dovetail joints (*page 71, Step 2*). Often the top dowels are press-fitted into their holes to avoid glue from dripping down the balusters.

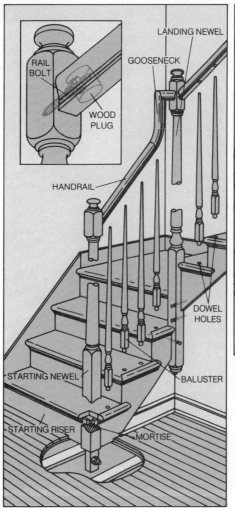

RAIL BOLT

WOOD PLUG

LANDING NEWEL

GOOSENECK

HANDRAIL

DOWEL HOLES

STARTING NEWEL

BALUSTER

STARTING RISER

MORTISE

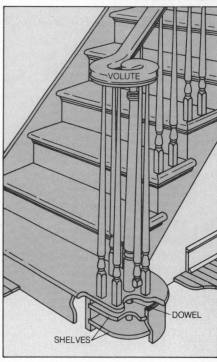

VOLUTE

DOWEL

SHELVES

A newel post in a bullnose tread. In an adaptation of a traditional form, many stairways use a longer starting tread, a bullnose, which simplifies newel-post installation. The post is set in a hole drilled through the center of the tread end, and a 1½-inch dowel extends to floor level through two shelves inside the curved riser. The spiraled end of the railing, the volute, is glued onto a dowel that protrudes up from the newel post. Balusters from the bullnose to the volute further support the rail.

Silencing a Squeaky Tread

Squeaks, a common problem in older, carriage-supported stairways (page 66), are caused by treads that rub against other stair parts when stepped on. The rubbing movement indicates that some portion of the tread has separated slightly from the carriage or the riser, because of warping or shrinking in these parts; the separated portion is pushed down by a footfall and then springs back up. You can stop tread spring by making the separated portion stay down, or by inserting a thin wedge as a shim underneath it.

First, locate the movement. Use a level to find warps, twists or bows. While a helper climbs the stairs, listen, watch for rise and fall and—resting your hand on the tread—feel for vibration.

After you find the spring, you can repair it if it is minimal with pairs of angled nails. If the tread movement is substantial, use wedges.

Such repairs from the top are usually sufficient. But if you can get to the stairway from underneath you can make a sound and simple fix, preferable because it is invisible, by adding glue blocks (opposite, top) to the joint between the tread and the riser under its front edge, the most common source of squeaks. If the tread is badly warped or humped in the center, rejoin it with a screw through the carriage (opposite, center).

Squeaks in modern housed-stringer stairways (page 67, top) are uncommon. If the squeak comes from between a tread and a riser, try nailing or wedging. If it comes from the end of the tread, the glue wedge that supports it has probably worked loose from shrinkage or the hammering of footfalls. If accessible, replace the wedge (opposite, bottom) with a new one from the lumberyard or a homemade one cut from 1-inch hardwood.

Working from Above

Nailing the tread down. Drive two eightpenny finishing nails into ³⁄₃₂-inch pilot holes drilled at opposing angles through the tread and into the riser at the point of movement. Have a helper stand on the tread during both drilling and nailing. If the squeak comes from the ends of the tread, angle the holes into the carriage. Sink the nails with a nail set and wood-putty the holes.

If the tread spring is too great for nails to close, fasten the tread with a No. 8 wood screw 2½ inches long driven through an 1¹⁄₆₄-inch shank hole in the tread and into a ³⁄₃₂-inch pilot hole in the riser (inset). Apply paraffin wax to the threads to make the screw turn easily in oak. Glue a piece of dowel into the countersink hole and sand it off level with the tread.

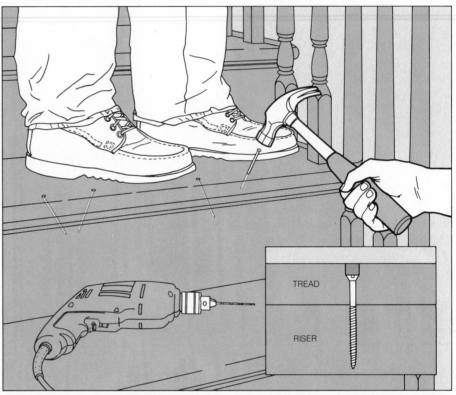

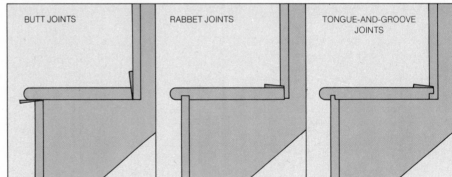

Wedging treads tight. Remove the scotia molding under the tread nose and insert a knife into the tread joints to discover the kind of joints used. If they are butt joints, the knife will slip vertically into the joint behind the tread and horizontally under the tread; if the knife-entry directions are reversed, the joints are either rabbet or tongue-in-groove (above, center and right). Drive sharply tapered wedges coated with glue into the cracks in the indicated directions.

Most wedges tighten a shrunken joint or force the tread down to the carriage, and should be driven hard. The wedge under the tread in a butt joint should prevent a bowed tread from moving by shimming it up; drive it just enough to stop the squeak without increasing the bow.

Cut wedges off with a utility knife and replace the scotia molding. The joints at the back of treads can be covered with shoe molding.

Working from Below

Installing glue blocks. Coat glue on two sides of a block of wood 1½ inches square and about 3 inches long, press it into the joint between the tread and the riser, and fasten the block with a nail in each direction. Add two or three more blocks. If the joint has old blocks that have come partly unstuck, either install new blocks between them, or pry them off, scrape the dried glue on the stair parts down to bare wood and use the new blocks as replacements.

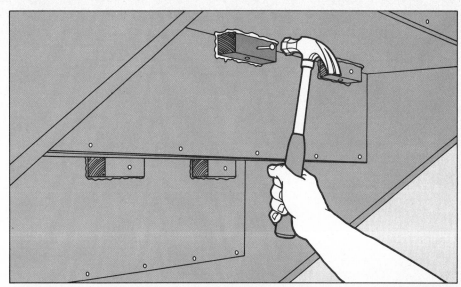

Installing a screw through the carriage. About 2 inches below the tread, chisel a shallow notch into the carriage and with a helper standing on the tread drill a ⅛-inch pilot hole angled at about 30° through the corner of the carriage and ¾ inch into the tread. Enlarge the hole through the carriage with a ¼-inch drill. Spread a bead of construction adhesive along both sides of the joint between the tread and the carriage, and, with the helper off the tread, work the adhesive into the joint, using a putty knife. Have the helper stand on the tread again and install a No. 12 wood screw 3 inches long.

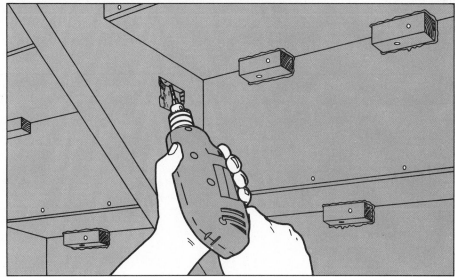

Wedges for a Prefab Stair

Replacing loose wedges. Split out the old wedge with a chisel, and pare dried glue and splinters from the notch. Plane a new wedge to fit within an inch of the riser. Coat the notch, the bottom of the tread and the top and bottom of the wedge with glue. Hammer the wedge snugly into the notch, tap it along the side to force it against the notch face, then hit the end a few more times to jam the wedge tightly under the tread.

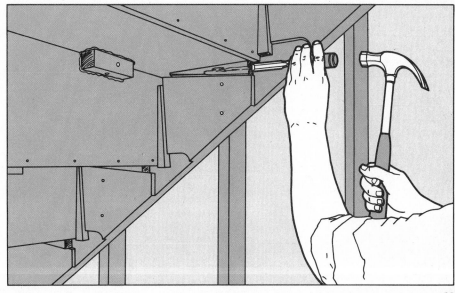

Repairing a Balustrade

With its graceful molded railing and its row of slender balusters, the stairway balustrade, essential for safety, is also the set piece of the cabinetmaker's art in most homes. Thus a broken baluster or a shaky railing affects not only the safety but also the appearance.

A baluster that is merely loose can be tightened with glue, nails or small wedges, but if it is cracked or badly scraped or dented, it should be replaced. Begin by determining how your balusters are fastened. Square-topped balusters usually join the railing by fitting into a shallow groove just as wide as the baluster is thick. Blocks of wood called fillets are nailed into the grooves between balusters. In some staircases such balusters may also end at the bottom in the groove of a lower rail, called a buttress cap, that lies on top of a stringer of uniform width nailed to the ends of the treads and risers (opposite page, Steps 1 and 2).

Turned balusters rounded clear to the top go into holes in the railing. At the bottom, if they do not overlap the return nosing (the piece that hides the end-grain of the tread), they are also doweled, even though they may have square ends. But square-ended balusters that land on the tread slightly overlapping the return nosing are probably joined to the tread by a dovetail joint, and you will have to remove the return nosing not only to be sure but also to make the replacement. Save the broken baluster and use it as a pattern for a new one. If you cannot find a match at a lumberyard, you will have to locate a cabinetmaker who will turn one. You can buy a square-bottomed replacement for a dovetailed baluster and cut the dovetail yourself, using the principles shown on page 74, but you can also simply pin a doweled baluster into the dovetailed tread with a nail.

The cause of a weak and wobbly railing is usually a bottom newel post with poor fastenings or loosely cut mortises for the riser and stringer. In carriage stairways the cure is to reinforce the post with a lag bolt driven into structural boards behind it. For posts in bullnose treads, you can run a bolt up through the floor into the foot of the post.

Replacing a Doweled Baluster

1 **Removing the damaged baluster.** Saw the baluster in two and sharply twist the bottom piece with a pipe wrench to break the glue joint at the base. Remove the top piece; if it is stuck or glued, use the wrench. If the joints do not break, saw the baluster flush, using cardboard on the tread to guard it from the saw. Drill out the dowel ends with spade bits the size of those on the new baluster.

With a folding rule held against the high edge of the dowel hole in the railing (inset), measure to the tread. Cutting from the top, shorten the new baluster to this length plus ½ inch. Saw the bottom dowel to a ³⁄₁₆-inch stub.

2 **Installing the new baluster.** Smear glue in the tread hole, angle the top dowel into the railing hole and pull the bottom of the baluster across the tread, lifting the railing about ¼ inch. Seat the bottom dowel in the tread hole. If the railing will not lift, bevel the top dowel where it binds against the side of the hole.

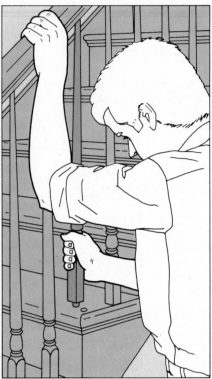

A Dovetailed Baluster

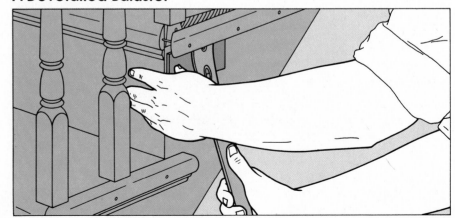

1 **Removing the return nosing.** Use a chisel to crack the joints, then insert a utility bar and pry off the return molding and return nosing. Protect the stringer with a pry block. Saw through the old baluster and hammer it out of the dovetail.

2 Nailing in the new baluster. Insert the top of a cut-to-length doweled baluster into the railing hole and set its base in the tread dovetail where the old baluster was, shimming behind the dowel if necessary. Drill a pilot hole through the dowel into the tread, and drive a nail through the hole. Replace the return nosing and return molding, driving finishing nails through the old holes, and putty over the nailheads.

A Filleted Baluster

1 Taking out the old baluster. With a chisel, split the fillets below the butt of the old baluster and above the top into several pieces and pry them out. Drive each end of the baluster toward the chiseled-out grooves, breaking the nailing, and remove the baluster. Scrape old glue from the grooves. Obtain the angle for the new baluster ends and fillets using a T bevel between an adjacent baluster and fillet. Mark the angle on the new baluster and saw it to length.

Tightening a Shaky Newel

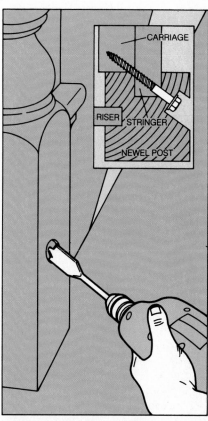

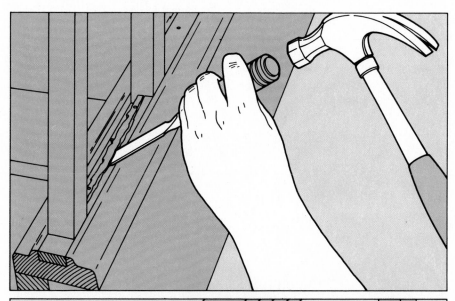

Installing a lag bolt. With a ¾-inch spade bit aimed at the carriage, drill a countersink hole ¾ inch deep in the newel post 4 inches up and centered. Extend it into the carriage with a $\frac{7}{32}$-inch bit and ream it out to $\frac{5}{16}$ inch through the newel. With a socket wrench, screw in a $\frac{5}{16}$-inch bolt 4 inches long fitted with a washer (*inset*). Plug the hole with a dowel.

To steady a newel set in a bullnose tread, start by driving two nails through the flooring short distances from the newel. From beneath, measure from the nail points to locate the bottom of the newel dowel. Drill shank and pilot holes and install a $\frac{5}{16}$-inch lag bolt 3 inches long. Pull the nails and wood-putty the holes.

2 Fastening the new baluster. Set the baluster against the existing fillets and toenail two finishing nails through each end—into the railing and buttress cap. Start the nails where the new fillets will hide them, and set the heads. Measure the length of each new fillet, mark the angle cuts with the T bevel and cut with a miter box. Coat the backs and sides with glue and attach them in the railing and buttress-cap grooves with fourpenny finishing nails.

Retreading a Stairway

Subject to heavy traffic, stair treads suffer scrapes, dents and stains, and may wear unevenly or split. In any type of stairway, you can readily replace individual treads, except for a bullnose starting tread, which requires dismantling the railing and replacing the newel post. The material for the replacement is standard lumberyard oak stair tread, $1\frac{1}{16}$ inches thick and $11\frac{1}{2}$ inches wide, which has a nosing milled onto the front edge.

In a housed-stringer stairway, you can replace a tread by chiseling out the wedges beneath it (page 69, bottom) and behind the riser above it, removing both parts, and wedging in a new tread and the old riser. If one end of the tread rests on an open stringer, as in the picture at the top of page 67, remove the balusters (pages 70-71), and hammer the tread and then the riser free from their nailings.

For a carriage-supported stairway that has one side open, follow the steps that begin on this page. For such a stairway closed on both sides, see page 75.

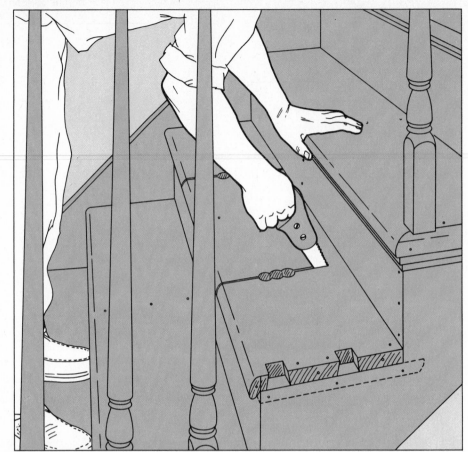

1 **Cutting up the old tread into thirds.** After taking off the balusters (pages 70-71) and the moldings, drill starting holes for a saw and cut across the tread in two places, nicking the edges of the risers in front and behind, but stopping the cut before damaging their exposed surfaces.

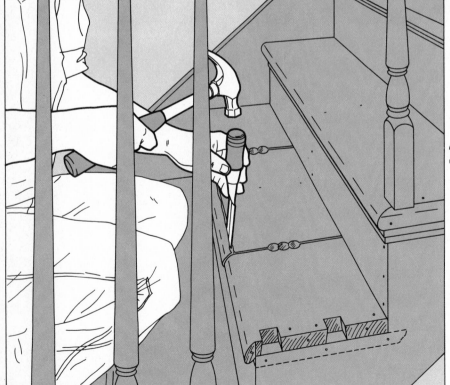

2 **Splitting out the sections.** Drive a chisel into the middle third over the riser, so that the nosing breaks off without damaging the riser tongue. Working backward over the middle carriage, split off more pieces. Pry the last inch or so gently away from the nails that hold it to the back riser. Hammer the chisel sideways into the ends of the other thirds, splitting around nails and baluster dowels, and pull out the pieces. Cut off all protruding nails.

Saw the new tread to length and wide enough to fit in the slot left, after you pulled out the tread end, between the side carriage and the skirt stringer above it. If your stairway has rabbet or tongue-and-groove joints between treads and risers, make allowance in trimming the tread to width and rout rabbets or tongues and grooves on the tread, or have a mill do it.

Putting In the New Tread: On an Open Stair

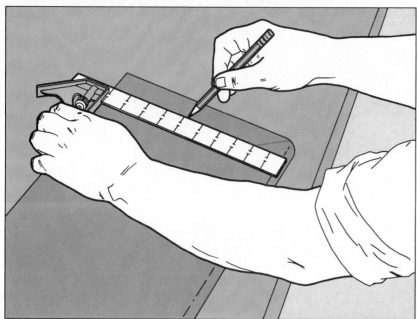

1 Laying out the nosing cuts. With a combination square, mark the cuts for the return nosing on the outside end of the new tread. First draw a 45° line in from the front corner of the tread for the miter cut, then lay out a crosscut the width of the nosing.

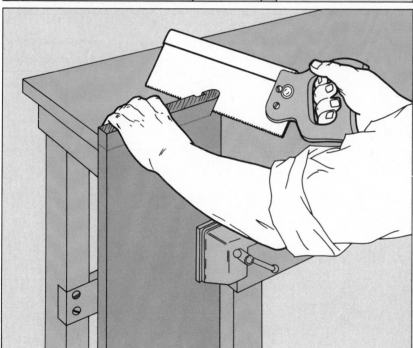

2 Sawing the cuts. Cut along the 45° line with a backsaw, then crosscut with a fine-toothed hand-saw or a saber saw held against a 1-by-2 guide clamped to the tread. Smooth the cuts with a block plane and a chisel.

3 Laying out dovetail mortises. With the tread temporarily in place, use a plumb bob to mark the point directly beneath the center of a railing hole. Angle the upper end of the baluster into the hole, hold the bottom against the tread end centered on the plumb-bob mark, and scribe the dovetail angles. With a square extend the lines onto the top and bottom of the tread, and connect them with lines as far in as the thickness of the dovetail. Repeat for the other baluster.

If the balusters are doweled into the treads, use the mark as the center for dowel holes.

4 **Sawing out the dovetails.** Cut the sides of the dovetails just inside the marks with a backsaw, then cut the back with a coping saw. Smooth the saw cuts by paring them with a chisel.

If the balusters are doweled, drill holes of the dowel diameter ⅜ inch deep, using a spade bit.

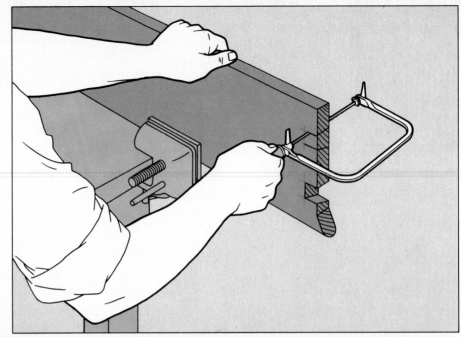

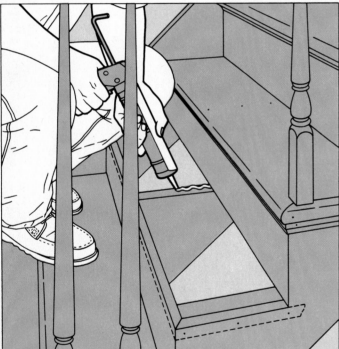

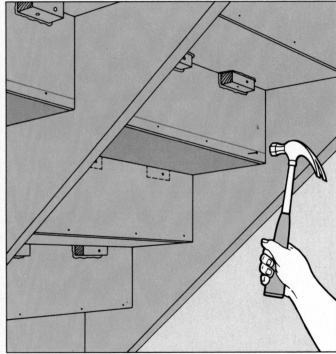

5 **Gluing down the new tread.** Check the tread against the carriages, and drill three ³⁄₃₂-inch pilot holes across the tread at each point where it will lie over a carriage. Spread generous beads of construction adhesive along the tops of the carriages, using a caulking gun. Slide the tread into place under the skirt-stringer. Drive eight-penny finishing nails through the pilot holes into the carriages; countersink the heads of the nails and fill the holes with wood putty. Keep traffic off the tread for three hours to let the adhesive set. Replace the balusters, the return nosing and the moldings, as shown on pages 70-71.

6 **Fastening from underneath.** If you can reach the underside of the stairway, drill pilot holes through the riser into the tread and drive eight-penny nails. Use glue blocks (*page 69*) along the joint between the tread and the riser below.

Putting In the New Tread: On a Closed Stair

1 **Finding the length of the new tread.** Measure from the face of one skirt-stringer across the stairway into the notch beneath the other. Subtract ⅛ inch to leave some play, and cut the new tread to this length. If the front riser was tongued or rabbeted into the old tread, chisel and plane it flush with the carriages.

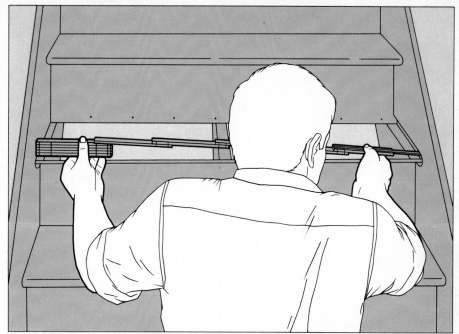

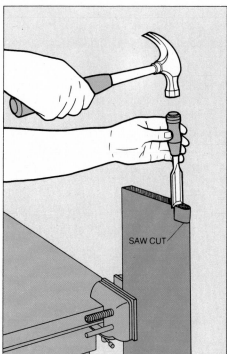

SAW CUT

2 **Notching the nosing.** Using a backsaw and a chisel, make a notch in one of the front corners of the new tread. The distance from the end of the tread to the saw cut should be equal to the depth of the slot under the skirt-stringer; the chisel split should be made as far back from the nosing as the amount of overhang of the tread above, plus ½ inch for play. Save the cutout scrap of nosing.

3 **Installing the tread.** Apply adhesive to the carriages and, holding the uncut end of the tread angled upward, insert the notched end beneath the skirt-stringer. The notch will allow you to pull the tread far enough forward to avoid hitting the nose of the tread above. Lower the other end to the carriages, push the tread tight against the back riser, then slide it sideways until the tread notch is revealed. With glue and a nail through a pilot hole, fasten the scrap of nosing into the tread notch. Center the tread, drill pilot holes and nail the tread down, toenailing at the ends if the carriages are under the stringers.

Opening the Floor for a New Stairway

If you can reach your basement only by trudging through rain and cold to an exterior door, if valuable attic storage space is accessible only by balancing on a chair, if you must tiptoe through an adjoining bedroom to get to an upstairs study—you know you need a stairway. The first step is to create an access hole in the upper floor—a stair opening with new framing to do the work of the structural members you cut out.

Since the addition of new stairs changes the layout of two floors, framing the opening requires forethought. Try to locate the stairs so that existing walls will not have to be removed or shifted to accommodate the new construction; most stairs, for instance, need clearance of at least 3 feet between the top or bottom tread and a facing wall in order to provide turning space for entering or leaving the stairs. Also try to position the new stairs to avoid interference with plumbing lines, electrical wiring and heating ducts. And if you can plan the stairs so the longer sides of the opening run parallel to the joists (below), you will simplify the framing.

Consult local building codes, which often specify minimum dimensions for clear passageway and headroom—factors that determine the minimum width and length of a stair opening. Some codes stipulate that main stairs provide an opening at least 32 inches wide between the handrails—stairs with two handrails, each occupying 3½ inches, would need an opening at least 39 inches wide. The opening must be even wider if its sides are finished with wood or wallboard.

The length of a stair opening also is governed by practical considerations. A conventional stair opening need only be long enough to provide adequate clearance overhead. A minimum of 76 inches is required by most codes for basement stairs and 80 inches for main stairs. Remember that the code requirement is a minimum. Greater clearance is advantageous—to accomodate tall people and to simplify the job of moving furniture.

How the opening is measured and marked depends on the type of stairway to be installed. For most types, follow the procedure for a cleat basement stairway (page 84); the instructions for a spiral stairway and a disappearing stairway are given on page 80. However, openings for all types of stairs are cut and reinforced in essentially the same way, following the basic techniques illustrated here for a basement stairway.

Cutting a stair opening requires the removal of some finish flooring, subflooring, joists and—for all but unfinished basements, shown here to simplify illustrations—sections of finished ceiling. Careful shoring is particularly important for an opening that runs perpendicular to joists. In this case, as many as six joists may have to be cut for a conventional stair, and posts or walls erected underneath as permanent supports for the uncut portions, called tail joists.

For a spiral stairway the opening must be finished before stair installation; in most other cases, finish work is done after installation. Use scraps of ceiling material to patch gaps around the stair opening. Special moldings called landing nosing, available from stairway manufacturers and at lumber-supply stores, can be installed around the upper edges of the opening if a balustrade will be installed (page 91). Otherwise, hide the exposed edges of plaster, plywood and finish flooring with decorative moldings.

Anatomy of a stair opening. For most openings parallel to joists, cut portions of two joists and fasten the cut ends, or tail joists, with joist hangers to doubled 2-by-10 headers. The header hangers are nailed to "trimmer joists" on the sides of the opening. On the right side of this example the trimmers consist of a new joist fastened to an existing one; on the left, two new trimmer joists have been installed between existing floor joists to narrow the width of the opening to the dimensions required for the stairway.

An opening across joists is made similarly but should run along a bearing wall that supports the trimmer joists. An opening along a foundation wall requires special techniques (page 79).

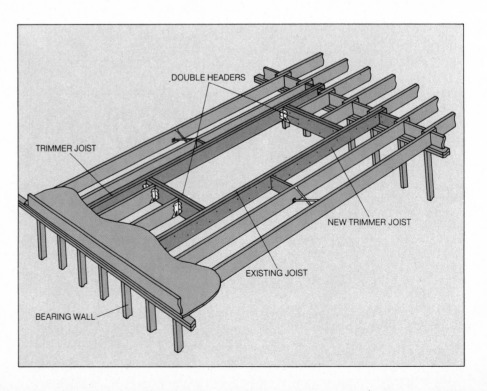

DOUBLE HEADERS

TRIMMER JOIST

NEW TRIMMER JOIST

EXISTING JOIST

BEARING WALL

1 **Supporting the floor.** Shoring must be erected. First mark the opening of the subfloor underside, locating it as described on page 85, Step 2, for most stairways and on page 80 for disappearing stairways and spiral stairways. Double joists on each side of the proposed hole *(page 17)* or triple them if they are to bear the weight of a partition wall above. Install the shoring *(pages 20-21)* beyond each end of the opening. Drill holes up through the floor at each corner.

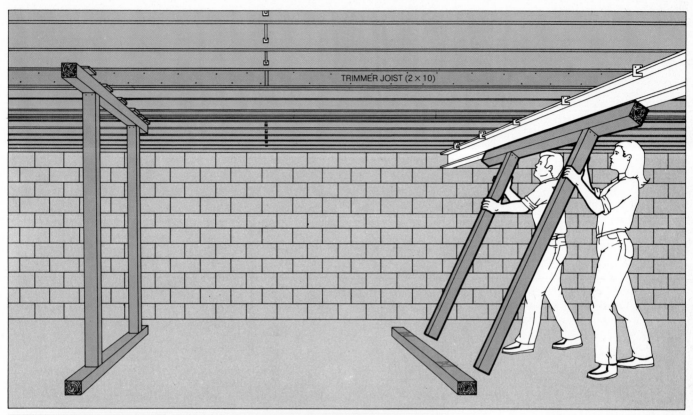

TRIMMER JOIST (2 × 10)

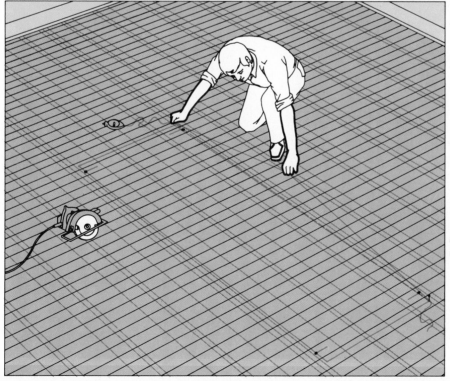

2 **Cutting the opening.** On the upper floor, locate the holes at the corners of the opening of the planned stair, extend the length of the opening 3 inches beyond each end to allow for the thickness of the double headers *(page 79, Step 5)*, and snap four chalk lines to mark out the extended opening. Saw through finish floor and subfloor along the two sides of the opening that are at right angles to the floorboards. Pry up the cut boards as shown on page 11. Then cut along the two sides parallel to the floorboards.

3 Removing the subfloor. To loosen the subfloor from the joists, you must pound upward with a 2-by-4 along the sides of each joist under the sawed section. Then use a pry bar from above to complete the job.

4 Cutting the joists. Hand-saw the joists flush with the opening while a helper supports each joist from underneath to prevent it from pinching the saw as you cut. The cut joists can then be used to make the double headers required to complete the framing *(drawing, page 76)*; cut two lengths to fit between the trimmer joists at each end of the opening and fasten them together with tenpenny nails in a W pattern.

5 **Installing the headers.** Nail 3-inch joist hangers to each end of a double header and butt the header side against the ends of the cut, or tail, joists, bringing its top edge level with the top of the trimmers and tail joists. Then nail the joist hangers to the trimmer joists using all nail holes in the hangers. Slip 1½-inch joist hangers onto the tail joists from below and nail them to the tail joists and the headers. Then install the other double header in the same way.

An Opening Next to a Foundation Wall

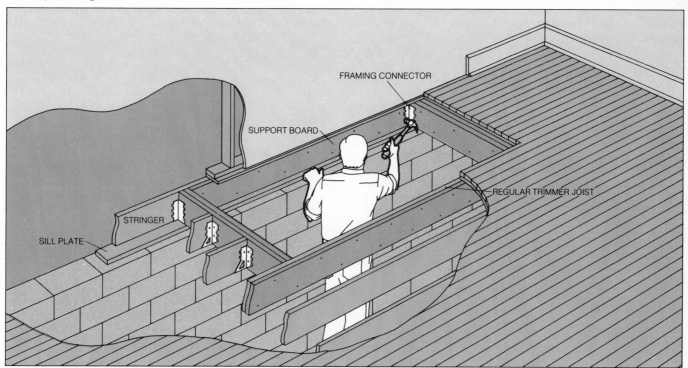

FRAMING CONNECTOR

SUPPORT BOARD

REGULAR TRIMMER JOIST

STRINGER

SILL PLATE

Setting the headers on the wall. If you are installing a basement stair alongside a masonry wall, add a support board to the stringer atop the wall to make one of your trimmer joists. First pound the headers—without joist hangers—against the regular trimmer, the cut tail joists and the stringer trimmer. Fasten the headers to the regular trimmer and tail joists as in Step 5. Use metal framing connectors to fasten the headers to the stringer joist and support board.

Two Spacesavers—Disappearing and Spiral Stairs

Not every home has enough space for a full flight of stairs to an attic or basement, or an additional flight between main floors. But even the most cramped floor plans can accommodate the two stairways shown below and at right and on pages 82-83. A disappearing stair pulls down from a ceiling to provide access to attic storage space, then folds back into the attic when not in use. A spiral stairway not only adds style and beauty to any room, but also takes 70 per cent less space than a regular stairway.

Disappearing stairs, usually made of unfinished softwoods, are sold as preassembled units by major retail chains and home-improvement centers. Most stairs, like the ones shown below and opposite, close manually into a double or triple fold; the folds are hinged to a wood frame and concealed behind a plywood ceiling panel. More complex models slide up and down on a pulley system or have an electric motor for automatic operation. Spiral stairs, of hardwood, aluminum or steel, are available in kits from several manufacturers, listed in classified directories and dealer catalogues under "Stair builders" and "Iron works."

Both disappearing and spiral stairs require stair-well openings *(pages 76-79)* made to the dimensions specified by the manufacturers. The folding attic stairs come in standard sizes to fit openings 25 to 30 inches wide and 54 to 60 inches long. If you make the opening parallel to the ceiling joists, you need cut only one joist to accommodate the stair; if you must cross the joists, you may have to cut as many as three framing members. In either situation, frame the opening with doubled joists and headers.

Before ordering a disappearing stair, measure the ceiling height and determine the clearance and attic headroom required for the model you have chosen. Clearance, which is measured horizontally on the floor directly beneath the opening, is the amount of space needed to unfold the stairs. Headroom is the free space needed above the ceiling for the supporting hardware and the handrail.

Ordering a spiral stair requires a few more measurements. First, determine the stair diameter and location best suited to your floor plans. Spiral kits come in a range of widths from 3 to 8 feet, but the minimum width is not recommended—carrying even small items is difficult on a stairway less than 4 feet wide. Find the most comfortable direction of entry and exit to and from the stairway on both floors, and decide whether you prefer a right-hand stair (climbed counterclockwise) or a left-hand one.

When ordering a spiral stairway, you must also specify the exact height of the stair from finished floor to finished floor. To get an accurate measurement, drill a ⅛-inch hole through the upper floor and drop a plumb bob to the floor below.

Draw a sketch to accompany your order, indicating the diameter and height of the stairway, the preferred entry and exit direction on each floor and the location of adjoining walls or other obstructions. The manufacturer will help you determine the number and size of treads for either a full spiral (360°) or a three-quarter turn (270°).

To strengthen the floor the stair will rest on, double the joists beneath the center pole *(page 76)*. If the center pole falls between joists, double the joists on either side and insert wood blocking *(page 17, Step 1)* between the doubled joists for reinforcement.

Before you begin the installation, mark the location of each tread on the center pole. Counting the landing as one tread, divide the floor-to-floor height in inches by the number of treads in the kit. For example, a kit that includes 12 treads and a landing and is intended for a total height of 104 inches should have its center pole marked for an 8-inch interval between steps. On a well-designed spiral stair, the rise should not be less than 7 inches or more than 9 inches.

Installing a Disappearing Stair

1 **Attaching the stair.** After cutting and framing an opening *(pages 76-79)* to fit the stair, bolt its frame to joists and headers with ⅜-by-4½-inch bolts. To hold it in place while drilling holes and inserting bolts, shim it level on top of two 2-by-4 braces, which are fastened to the double joists by nails driven through the ceiling and removed after the stair is installed.

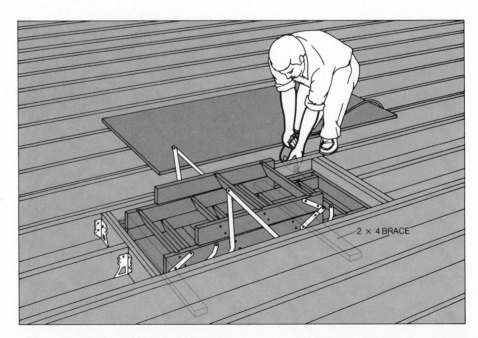

2 × 4 BRACE

2 **Cutting the side rails to size.** Pull the stair from the stair box, unfold the middle section and, following the angle of the stair, measure the distances from the front and rear edges of this section to the floor. Mark the side rails of the bottom section with these measurements—be sure not to reverse the distances—and draw cutting lines, indicated here by a broken line, between the marks. Saw along the lines on each side rail and smooth the cuts with sandpaper.

A Stairway with a Twist

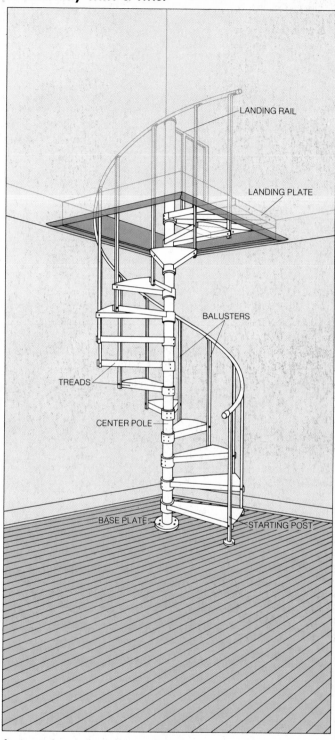

Anatomy of a spiral stair. This typical metal staircase, which comes in a kit, consists of a center pole mounted on a base plate and 12 treads secured to the post and braced at their outer edges by 12 balusters. A landing plate and a landing rail top the stairs; a starting post at the bottom forms the starting point for a curving handrail made either of plastic or metal.

Assembling and Installing a Spiral Stairway

1 **Positioning the center pole.** Stretch two strings diagonally from nails driven into opposite corners of the well hole. Drop a plumb line from the intersection of the strings to the floor below and then mark the spot where the plumb bob touches the floor.

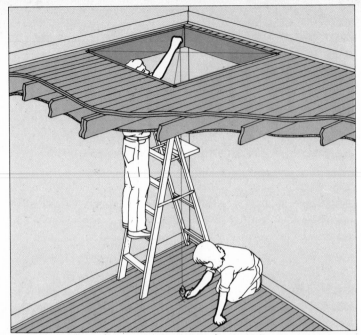

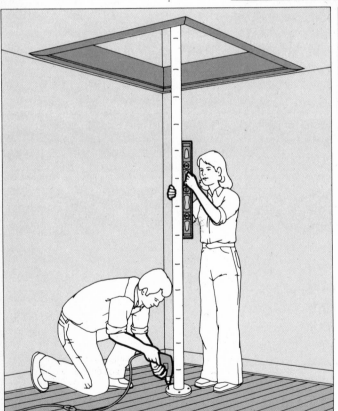

2 **Securing the pole.** Stand the center pole on the floor mark—be sure it is both centered and plumb—and using the predrilled holes in the base plate as a guide, drill pilot holes into the subflooring for the lag bolts provided with the kit. On a concrete floor, drill the holes with a masonry bit and insert expansion anchors for the lag bolts. Then slide all the treads, faceup, to the bottom of the center pole.

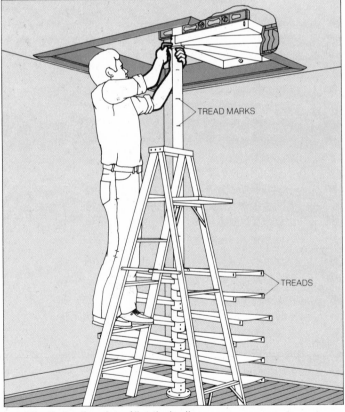

3 **Installing the landing plate.** Align the landing plate with the top tread mark and, while a helper levels the plate, insert the four setscrews into the hub and tighten them loosely against the center pole. Drill pilot holes through the landing-plate flanges into a joist and header of the hole framing and fasten the landing plate to the framing with lag bolts. Make a final leveling adjustment, then tighten the setscrews.

TREAD MARKS

TREADS

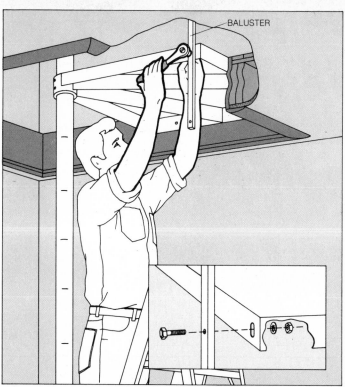

BALUSTER

4 **Bolting the first baluster.** Align the upper hole of a baluster with the predrilled hole in the landing-plate flange. Then fasten the baluster to the landing plate with a nut, bolt and washer furnished with the kit *(inset)*.

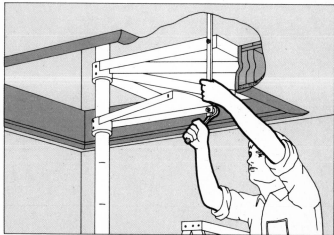

5 **Setting the first tread.** Align the top tread with the top tread mark, and the hole at the back of this tread with the open hole in the installed baluster; then level the tread and bolt it to the baluster, as in Step 4. Tighten the four setscrews in the tread hub. Repeat the procedure down to the floor, fastening each tread to the one below it with the balusters. At the base of the stair, bolt the starting post to the bottom tread and secure the post to the floor with lag bolts, as in Step 2.

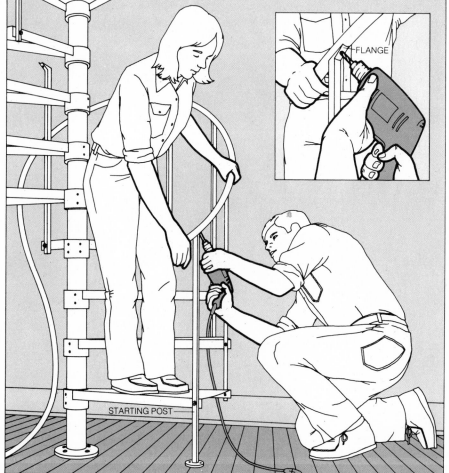

FLANGE

STARTING POST

6 **Installing the handrail.** Set the plastic handrail over the starting post and the first baluster, leaving a 2-inch overhang beyond the post. Then, using the predrilled flanges on the starting post and baluster as guides *(inset)*, mark and drill pilot holes into the underside of the handrail. Fasten the rail to both the post and baluster with the self-tapping screws that are in the kit. Proceed up the stair, unwinding the rail as you go and marking each hole before drilling; allow a 2-inch overhang beyond the top baluster and saw off the excess rail.

Bolt the landing plate to both the landing and the center pole, and install the caps that cover the ends of the handrail and the top of the pole.

83

Building Simple Basement Stairways Step by Step

Ancient builders knew the secret of comfortable stairs thousands of years ago, and modern carpenters use the same principles: for comfortable ascent or descent, a precise ratio must be maintained between the distance a person moves forward and the distance he raises or lowers himself. Today builders think in terms of "unit-rise" and "unit-run" to figure the ratio. Unit-rise is the vertical distance between the tops of successive treads; unit-run is the horizontal distance between the back edges of the treads. Adding all the units of rise gives the total rise; the total run is the sum of all the units of run. In any stairs there is one less unit-run than unit-rise because the top tread is actually the upper floor.

For any kind of stairway—the economical basement or patio stairs on page 87 or the finished main stairs shown on pages 88-90—carpenters make sure that the sum of the unit-run and unit-rise falls between 17 and 18 inches. Since stairs should not be as steep as ladders or as shallow as ramps, they keep the unit-rise between 6 and 9 inches. Many building codes go even further. The Federal Housing Authority, for example, requires a unit-run of at least 9 inches and a unit-rise of no more than 8¼ inches for most stairs, 9 inches for a basement stair.

Most codes also require nosings (page 66) of ½ to 1⅛ inches on each tread, giving more footroom. Headroom, measured from the finish-ceiling height down to the nose of a tread, is important as well; generally codes require at least 80 inches for most stair wells, or 76 inches for basement stairs.

Two common types of rough stairs are named for the way the treads are attached to the support boards. In a cleat stair, the treads rest on small blocks, or cleats, fastened to the inside faces of the supports, called stringers. In a cutout stair, the treads lie on notches cut into the supports, here called carriages. Use 2-by-10s for stringers and 2-by-12s for carriages. Use preservative-treated lumber for all parts of an outdoor stair and for supports of an indoor stair built against an unfinished foundation wall.

Stringers or carriages are anchored to the stair-well header at the top and to the floor at the bottom with framing connectors—steel brackets that can be adjusted by bending to hold boards together at any angle. When the lower floor is concrete, a kick plate, or small sill, is used instead and the bottoms of the supports are dabbed with wood preservative. Stringers or carriages are further anchored by nailing them to an adjacent

wall or by resting them on 2-by-4 posts.

Treads for a stair can be cut from any lumber but you can buy special tread stock, 9½ or 11½ inches wide and rounded on one edge for the nosing. Whatever wood is used, treads should be at least 1¹⁄₁₆ inches thick for stringers up to 30 inches apart; 1½-inch treads will span up to 36 inches. Add a middle cutout carriage for wider stairs. Risers, the vertically mounted boards that close the spaces between the treads, are usually cut from 1-by-8s or 1-by-10s to be as long as the treads and as wide as the unit-rise.

A framing square, a tool that resembles two rulers joined at a right angle, simplifies laying out stringers or carriages. Placed properly on a board (Step 3), the square quickly locates the necessary end cuts and tread positions. But you must be precise—use a sharp pencil.

Handrails, 30 to 34 inches above the tread nosings, are essential along any open portion of a stairway and are advisable along closed portions. For rough stairs, 2-by-3s bolted to the open side of the carriage or stringer serve as posts for 2-by-3 handrails. Screw them to the post and to the inside trimmer joist of the stair opening. Along a wall, use widely available wall rail brackets to support a 2-by-3 or a stock-molded handrail.

Preparing the Supports

1 **Determining the rise and run.** Measure between the upper and lower finish floors, or measure to the subfloor and account for the thickness of unlaid finish floors—8 feet 1 inch total in this example. You can measure by drilling a hole through the stair-well area. Convert the distance to inches (97 in this example), and divide by seven to get the number of risers. Round fractions up for a slightly shallower stair, down for a steeper one. Now divide the number of risers, here 13, into the total rise, 97 inches. The result is 7⁶⁄₁₃, the unit-rise. Since the unit-run—which excludes the nosing width—plus the unit-rise should total 17 to 18 inches, the unit-run can be between 9⁷⁄₁₃ and 10⁷⁄₁₃ inches. Choose a middle distance, here 10 inches; the total run will be 12 times 10 inches—120 inches.

Mark the lower floor directly beneath the place where the stringers' upper ends will rest. Measure the total run and mark the floor.

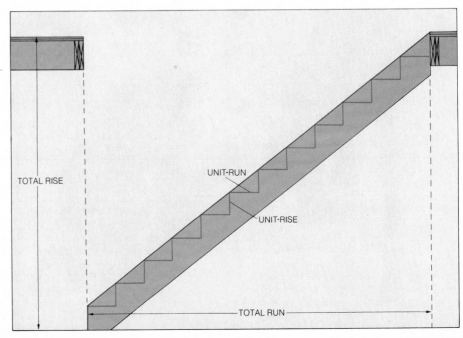

TOTAL RISE

UNIT-RUN

UNIT-RISE

TOTAL RUN

2 Marking the stair opening. Draw the first treads and risers on the wall, or, in the case of a stair that is in the middle of a room, on the floor. Measure down from the joists or ceiling to the nose of the treads beginning at the bottom. When you reach a tread mark at which the distance from ceiling to tread nose is less than minimum headroom, go to the next lower tread mark and mark the ceiling above with a plumb bob—this point indicates one end of the stair opening.

3 Marking the floor line. Place a framing square so the unit-run measurement, read on one outer scale, intersects the edge of the support board—using a 2-by-10 for a stringer, a 2-by-12 for a carriage. Shift the square until the unit-rise, read on the outer scale of the other leg, intersects the same edge of the board. Here the unit-rise is 7⅝₃; the unit-run is 10 inches. Draw a line around the outer edges of the square. Then extend the unit-run line across the board to mark the floor line.

NOSE

TREAD

TOTAL RUN MARK

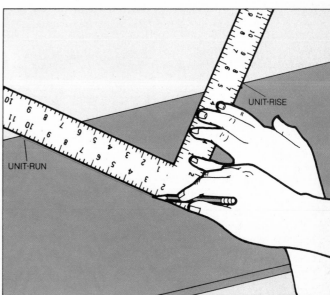

UNIT-RISE

UNIT-RUN

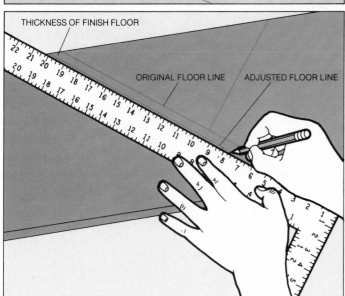

THICKNESS OF FINISH FLOOR

ORIGINAL FLOOR LINE   ADJUSTED FLOOR LINE

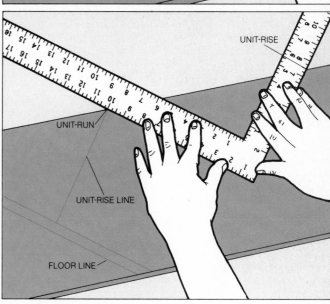

UNIT-RISE

UNIT-RUN

UNIT-RISE LINE

FLOOR LINE

4 Adjusting for a finish floor. To allow for the thickness of an unlaid finish floor with a cleat stair, shift the measured floor line toward the end of the board a distance equal to the thickness of the finish floor. Position the cleats to account for the thickness of the treads. To make a similar adjustment in a cutout stair, move the floor line down the thickness of the finish floor, then up the thickness of a tread; the result usually is an adjusted floor line slightly above the original.

5 Marking the tread lines. Slide the framing square up the support so that the unit-run measurement, read on one outer scale, is at the end of the first unit-rise line. Make certain the unit-rise measurement, read off the other leg of the square, is also at the edge of the board, and then mark around the square. The unit-run line is the tread line. Repeat the operation, moving the framing square up the board to mark unit-run and unit-rise lines for each step.

6 **Marking the header line.** Mark the last unit-run, or tread, and unit-rise lines as on page 85, Step 5. Then extend the unit-rise line down to the lower edge of the board to mark the line where the support will meet the stair-opening header. Check that the units of rise are of equal size, differing by no more than ¼ inch, then cut the board along the adjusted floor line, first unit-rise line and header line. If the stair is to be set over a kick plate on a concrete floor, cut out a 1½-by-3½-inch notch in the bottom front of the board to receive the kick plate (*Step 2*).

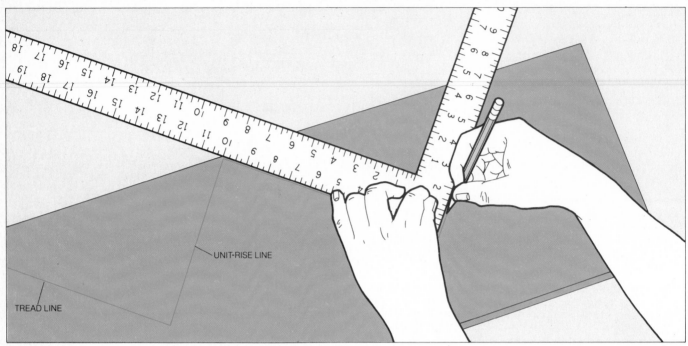

UNIT-RISE LINE

TREAD LINE

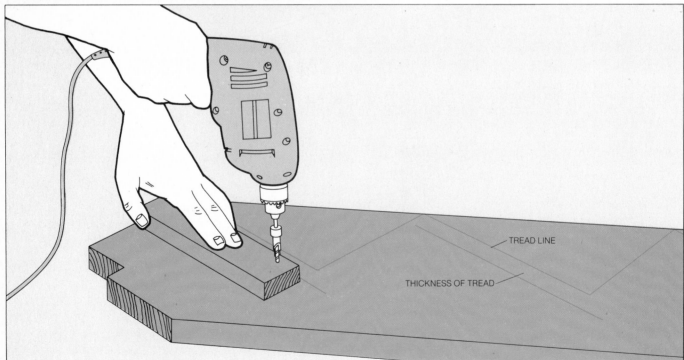

TREAD LINE

THICKNESS OF TREAD

7 **Finishing the support.** For a cleat stair (*above*), draw a line below each tread line at a distance equal to the thickness of a tread. Place the top of a 1-by-3 cleat, cut to the length of the unit-run, along each new line except in the top one, and use a counterbore bit for drilling pilot holes. Use five screws to secure each cleat. For a cut stair, saw along the tread lines and unit-rise lines, making certain not to cut any deeper into the support board than necessary.

Installing the Supports

1 Securing a support to the header. After tacking the top of the support in place against the header and checking to see that the tread lines are level, secure the top of the support with a framing connector. Bend the end of one leg of the connector to fit the bottom of the header *(inset)*. Use a center punch to make additional nail holes in a joist hanger if the framing connector overlaps one at the header. In a cleat stair, fasten the top cleat to the stringer.

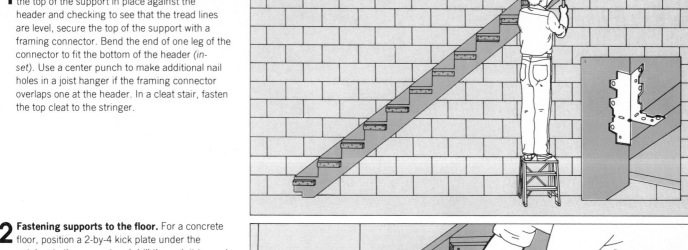

2 Fastening supports to the floor. For a concrete floor, position a 2-by-4 kick plate under the notches in the support and drill through it to mark the concrete. Then set it aside and use a masonry bit to drill holes for lead anchors. Replace the plate, fasten it with lag bolts and washers and toenail the supports to it.

For a wood floor, where a kick plate is not necessary, use a framing connector to fasten the support to the floor.

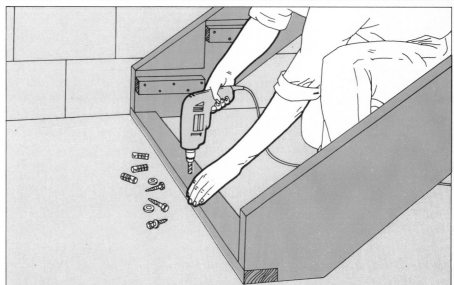

3 Bracing the supports. A support running along a wall is nailed to it, using masonry nails for foundations, tenpenny nails for studs; however, an open stairway requires posts as sketched at right. Secure a 2-by-4 plate to the floor beneath the support board with nails or bolts and anchors. Hold a 2-by-4 plumb on the plate, and mark it for an angle cut along the lower edge of the support. Cut the 2-by-4 along this line, then toenail it to the plate and stringer or carriage.

For a cleat stair, cut treads to fit between the stringers, then nail them in place, angling the nails so that they enter the stringer as well as the cleats. For a cutout stair, nail risers to the carriages first. Then butt the treads against the risers and nail them to the carriages.

SUPPORT POST

PLATE

A Craftsman's Pride: The Prefab Stair and Railing

To replace a main stairway or make an attractive passageway to a newly finished basement or attic, you may want something more elaborate than the simple stairs that are shown on the preceding pages. The best solution, handsome but economical, is a factory-built stairway with a graceful balustrade that you can assemble yourself from stock parts.

The stair builder will make a stairway to your specifications and, usually two to six weeks after you place your order, deliver the finished unit to your home. You must prepare the opening in the upper floor *(pages 76-79)* and, with two or three helpers, secure the stair to the opening and to the adjoining walls. Then, with the stair in place, you can fit the balustrade to it. This is the trickiest, most time-consuming part of the job: the intricate joinery of a balustrade requires not only skill in the use of professional wood-working tools but also the patience and perfectionism of a fine craftsman.

Ordering the stair correctly is the crucial first step. Some builders have local representatives who will help you to choose a stair and write the specifications for it, though even when this service is available it is your responsibility to be sure the installation will comply with local building codes. If you order the stair yourself, you must tell the manufacturer the total rise, total run and width of the stair. Measure the rise and estimate the run by the method shown on page 84, Step 1; the total run of the stair you receive may be slightly longer or shorter than your estimate, but your calculation will tell you roughly where the bottom of the stair will fall. Minimum stair widths are set by local codes *(page 76)*.

The stair builder must also know whether the stair will be fully or partially open, and whether the open side will be supported by a wall, as in the picture below. A free-standing open side must be strengthened, and any open side must have a balustrade. For a stair enclosed by walls, screw handrails to the wall framing. If you must install a balustrade, simplify the job by using a bullnose starting tread; the starting newel will fit into a

Installing the Stairway

1 **Fitting the stair in the opening.** Station a helper on the upper floor and walk the stair into position, with the housed stringer flush to the wall and the top riser against the double header; to hold the stair in position, temporarily nail two 2-by-4 blocks to the flooring in front of the bullnose starting tread. Use shims as necessary beneath the bullnose until the treads are level and the top of the top riser is exactly flush with the surface of the subflooring on the upper floor.

TOP RISER

HEADER

HOUSED STRINGER

BULLNOSE

hole drilled in the bullnose without the intricate cuts required for a landing newel. From the landing newel, a landing rail must run along all the unwalled sides of the stair opening.

Along with the stairway itself, the builder will provide a landing tread for the transition between the top of the stair and the finish floor. The parts of a balustrade—the gooseneck, volute, newel posts, balusters and handrail—must be ordered separately. You will also need finish moldings to conceal joints and shims, rail bolts (page 67) to join railing sections to each other and to a landing newel, and hardwood plugs to fill the access holes for the rail bolts.

The type of gooseneck you order depends on your local building code. A gooseneck leads a stair rail, usually set 30 inches above the tread nosing, up to the height of the landing rail, either 34 or 42 inches above the finish floor. If your code calls for a 34-inch landing rail, use a "one-riser" gooseneck as shown on page 92; the higher rail requires a longer "two-riser" gooseneck.

A spiral volute, supported by a starting newel and several balusters (page 67), is a common and attractive treatment for the lower end of the handrail; alternatives include a turn in the rail or a straight section called a starting easing. Some builders will attach these fittings to the handrail at the mill, but goosenecks must always be fitted on the job.

To get a good fit for the balustrade, you shound rent, borrow or buy several specialized woodworking tools. The hole for the starting newel calls for a heavy-duty ½-inch drill and a bit called a ship auger, 14 inches long and 1½ inches in diameter. A steel square and a pitch block—a wood triangle cut to the dimensions of a tread and riser (page 92)—are necessary to calculate the gooseneck dimensions; a precision miter box is essential for making accurate cuts on the rail and gooseneck. A router will make the landing-newel cuts faster and more accurately than a chisel, and a 4-foot level will help you to plumb balusters and newels and adjust handrail heights.

Finally, a caution on woodworking technique: to avoid splitting hardwood parts, always drill a pilot hole before driving a nail or screw. In some cases, as with the riser fastening in Step 2 (below), pilot holes should be drilled before positioning the stair (Step 1).

2 **Fastening the riser to the header.** If the header is plumb and perpendicular to the adjoining wall, fasten the top riser directly to the header with three horizontal rows of 16-penny finishing nails, spaced 10 inches apart horizontally and 2 inches vertically. If the header is out of plumb or square, tap wood shims between riser and header before nailing, using a combination square to be sure the shimming does not force the riser out of plumb with the tread beneath.

3 **Securing the housed stringer.** Locate and mark the positions of the wall studs behind the housed stringer and fasten the underside of the stringer to the center of each stud with two 16-penny common nails.

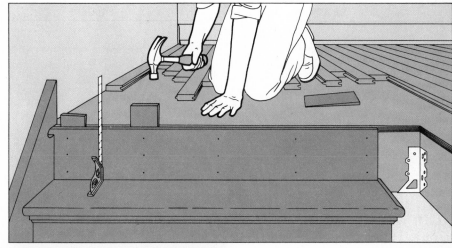

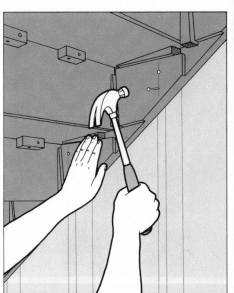

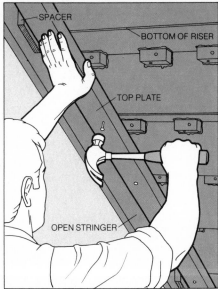

4 **Building a supporting wall.** Under the stair, tack ½-inch plywood spacers to the inner face of the open stringer at 3-foot intervals, then nail a 2-by-4 top plate to the risers with eightpenny nails; position the end of the plate on the floor and its outer edge flush to the spacers. Install a sole plate on the finish floor directly underneath, and complete the framing of the wall with studs between the sole plate and top plate. Remove the spacers and install wallboard, concealing the tops of the wallboard panels behind the stringer.

Assembling the Balustrade

1 **Marking the bullnose.** Cut out the printed paper template supplied by the manufacturer, place it on the bullnose tread with its cutout corner fitted to the corner of the riser and push the tip of an awl through the template and into the tread to mark the centers of the newel post and the bullnose balusters.

2 **A hole for the starting newel post.** Drill a vertical hole through the bullnose tread and shelves, using a heavy-duty ½-inch electric drill and a 1½-inch auger bit. To make sure that the hole is perfectly plumb, have helpers sight the bit against two combination squares (*below*); drill in short bursts, adjusting the angle of the bit between

bursts according to your helpers' instructions. Slide the dowel into the hole until the base of the newel rests on the tread. If the dowel is too long, cut it back; if it is too thick, then sand it down until it fits easily. If the newel is still not perfectly plumb, enlarge one side of the hole with the auger bit and shim.

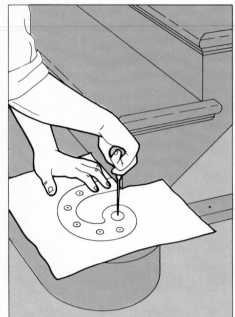

3 **Installing the newel.** Apply about a pint of glue to the drilled hole and the dowel, reset the newel into the bullnose, and get the newel exactly plumb with a 4-foot level while a helper nails braces to newel, stringer and the nosing of the second tread. Allow 24 hours for the glue to set. If you have easy access to the underside of the subfloor, drive a lag bolt up through the subfloor into the end of the dowel, using the techniques described on page 71.

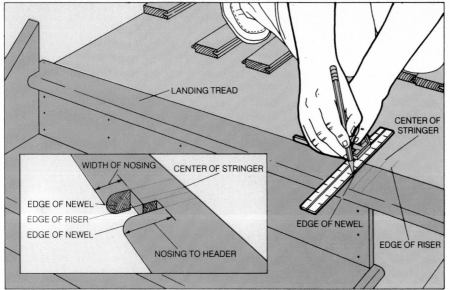

4 **Notching the landing tread.** Using a combination square, mark the landing subfloor in line with the outer edge of the top riser and the center of the open stringer, then slide the end of the landing tread into the matching notch in the housed stringer, set the tread in place on the top riser and transfer the marks to the tread. Across the tread, draw additional lines, centered on the stringer mark, to indicate the edges of the landing newel.

Measure the width of the tread nosing and the distance from the front of the nosing to the header; transfer both of the measurements to the face of the tread *(inset)*. Shade the area that must be notched, cut it out and then fasten the landing tread to the subfloor and headers with eightpenny finishing nails.

5 **Laying out the landing newel.** Using the dimensions provided by the manufacturer, mark a finish-floor line across the back and sides of the newel *(top)*. To locate this mark, measure down the newel from the point where the top of the gooseneck will meet the front of the newel to the point where the finish floor will meet the newel. On the newel bottom *(lower picture)*, measuring from the front, mark lines for the width of the landing tread nosing *(Step 4)* and for the distance from nosing to header; then measuring from the open side of the newel, mark a line for the edge of the riser *(Step 4)*.

Use a combination square to extend the nosing and header lines up the sides of the newel to the finish-floor line and, with a router or a chisel and mallet, cut away the wood in the shaded area from the bottom of the newel to the finish-floor line. Smooth the cuts with a plane.

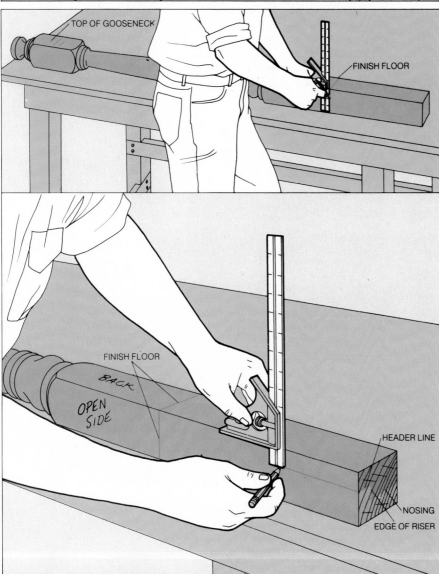

6 **Fitting the newel to the stringer.** On the stairway, measure the distance from the top of the landing tread to the tread below it and, measuring down the newel from the finish-floor line (*Step 5*), mark a tread line at this distance on all sides of the newel. Extend the riser line up the front of the newel to the tread line and shade the area that must be removed to allow the newel to fit over the stringer. Cut away the wood in the shaded area, then set the newel in position on the tread below the landing, pushing it tight against the riser; mark the return nosing flush with the front of the newel. Cut the return molding and nosing along the line you have just drawn so that the newel can lie flush against the stringer (*inset*). Set the post in place to check whether it fits properly; plane the cuts until the post rests snugly against the riser, stringer and cutouts in the landing tread. Then securely fasten the post to the header and stringer with countersunk wood screws or lag bolts.

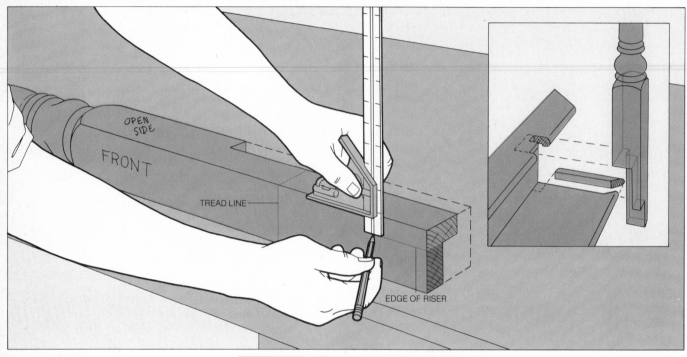

7 **Cutting the bottom of the gooseneck.** Prepare a pitch block—a right-angle triangle of wood with sides that are equal to the unit-rise and unit-run of the stairs—and have your helper hold a framing square upright with the block in its corner, run side down. Set the vertical part of the gooseneck tight against the tongue of the framing square and mark the point where the pitch block touches the gooseneck (*right*).

Set the rise side of the pitch block on a workbench alongside the framing square, hold the gooseneck against the tongue and, using the block as a straightedge, extend the mark into a line across the railing (*far right*). Cut the gooseneck along this line in an adjustable miter box.

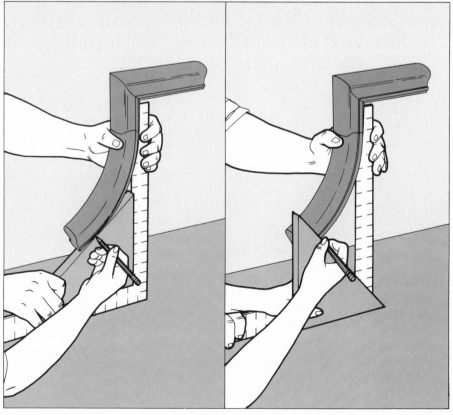

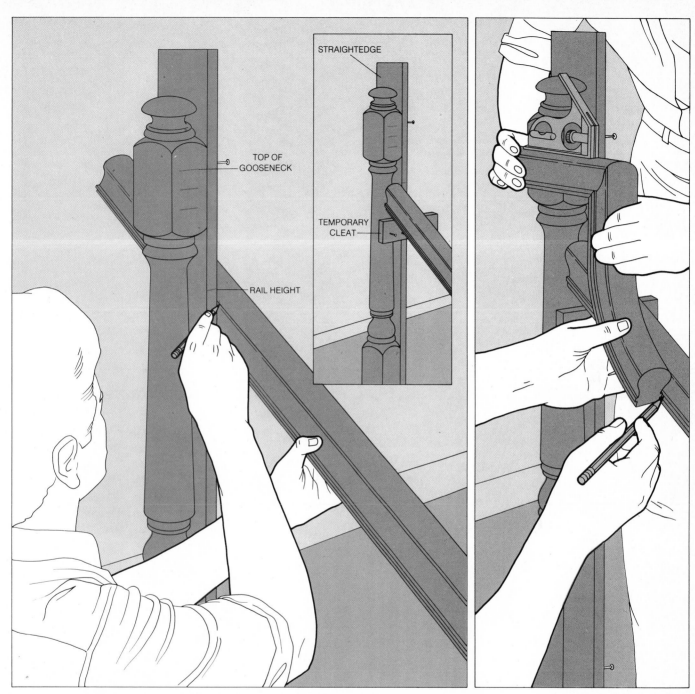

8 **Bracing the rail in place.** Nail a straight piece of 1-inch lumber to the side of the landing newel, with its front edge flush to the front of the newel. Measuring up from the landing-tread nosing, mark the straightedge at the rail height specified by your building code. Set the volute onto the dowel of the starting newel and, holding the upper end of the rail along the landing newel at the marked height and using the straightedge as a guide, draw a vertical line across the rail. Cut the rail along this line and with a combination square, align its top with the mark on the straightedge (inset). Position the rail with a temporary cleat nailed to the straightedge and newel.

9 **Cutting the rail.** Have a helper hold the gooseneck alongside the landing newel at the correct height above the finish floor (Step 5), with about 6 inches of the horizontal gooseneck section in front of the newel. Level the horizontal section with a combination square (above) or torpedo level, then mark where the bottom of the gooseneck intersects the rail. Use a miter box to cut the rail at the mark at a 90° angle.

10 **Installing the rail bolt.** Clamp the gooseneck in a vise, with the end of the curved section vertical, and drill a horizontal ¼-inch hole in this end; locate the hole 1⁵⁄₁₆ of an inch above the bottom of the gooseneck and drill it 1⅞ inches deep. Drill a matching ⅜-inch hole in the rail (*inset*). Mark the center of the railing bottom 1⅜ inches from the end and drill a hole at this point 1 inch wide and 1½ inches deep.

Screw the lag-threaded end of a rail bolt into the gooseneck; to tighten it, run the nut on the bolt to the end of its thread and turn it with an adjustable wrench. Remove the nut and washer and insert the other end of the bolt into the hole at the end of the rail. Run the washer and nut onto the bolt through the hole in the rail bottom and tighten the nut with a nail set.

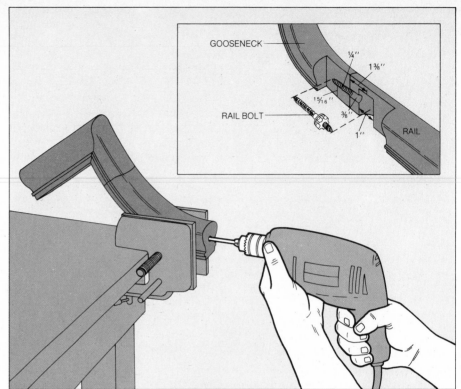

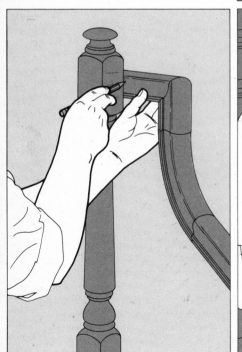

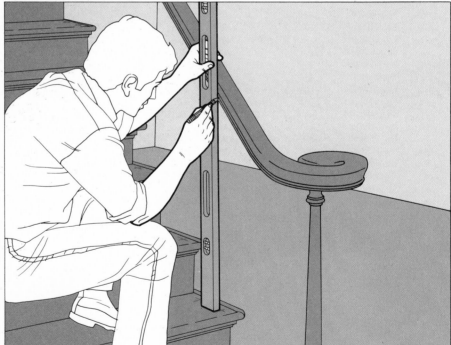

11 **Fitting the gooseneck to the newel.** Set the volute on the starting newel, hold the gooseneck alongside the landing newel at the correct height, and mark the point where the gooseneck meets the newel. Unbolt the gooseneck and cut it at this mark, then refasten the gooseneck and cut its end back in ⅛-inch increments until it fits snugly against the newel. Fasten the gooseneck to the newel with a rail bolt.

12 **Locating the balusters.** On each tread above the starting tread, mark the center line of the stringer and locate points for two baluster holes along this line, with the front of the first baluster directly over the front of the riser below the tread and the second halfway between the back of the first baluster and the front of the riser above the tread. Using a 4-foot level, plumb up from the marks to make corresponding marks on the railing side, then use a combination square to transfer the marks to the underside. Mark the underside of the volute with the paper template supplied by the stairbuilder (*Step 1*).

Using spade bits matched to the dowels at the bottom and top of the balusters, drill holes ¾ inch deep into the treads, and 1 inch deep into the volute and railing.

13 **Cutting the balusters to size.** Using a folding rule with a brass extension, measure the distances from the treads to the tops of the holes in the railing and cut the balusters to these lengths. Number the balusters, counting down from the top of the stairway. Loosen the bolt that fastens the gooseneck to the newel and, working down the stairway, try each baluster in place. If the top does not fit the hole in the rail, sand it down; if the baluster forces the rail out of line, shorten it ⅛ inch at a time.

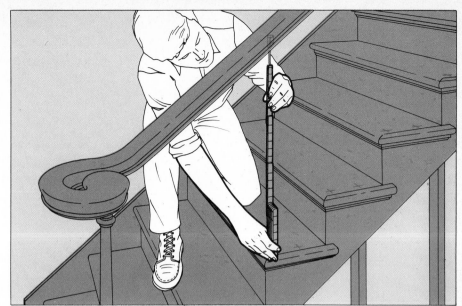

14 **Installing the balustrade.** Starting at the top of the stairway, lightly smear the top and bottom of each baluster with glue, apply a generous quantity to the hole in the tread, and insert balusters in the holes while a helper raises the railing at the volute. Work downward in groups of about six balusters at a time; after inserting each group, set a 2-by-4 block on the railing above it and strike it several times with a mallet. At the bottom of the stairway, coat the dowel on the starting newel with glue, install all of the balusters in the bullnose, and drive the volute down onto the newel and balusters.

Glue the joints on both sides of the gooseneck, tighten the rail bolts and toenail the joints together. Plug the holes beneath the rail bolts with cross-grained wood dowels.

Tightening carpet the modern way. The metal knee-kicker at center forces carpet onto a so-called tackless strip installed along the base-boards of a room. Everywhere else in a room, the carpet rests upon the rough waffled side of a sheet of padding; the smooth quilted side of the padding (*top right*) should face the floor.

Wall-to-wall carpeting, once a luxury reserved for the rich, is available to everyone now. Synthetic materials and new tools have made it so easy and inexpensive to install that it has become the flooring of choice in many new homes and apartments. And with good reason. Carpeting is safe and warm, soft and colorful. It soaks up sound. It camouflages defects in a floor and it can be laid over almost any surface without special preparation. Maintenance is simple: cleaning is a matter of regular vacuuming and occasional shampooing; stains can be removed with common cleaning agents; and most kinds of damage can be repaired at home.

As a decorative element, carpet is the most versatile of floorings. It works well in any room, even a kitchen or a bathroom, and comes in a variety of fibers. Wool, the oldest of all, is warm, handsome, long-wearing—and expensive. It is more difficult to clean than man-made fibers, and unlike them, can irritate allergies; moreover, it tends to build up charges of static electricity. Among the synthetics, acrylic most nearly resembles wool and is much less expensive. It wears well and produces little static. Nylon is popular for its strength, its color and the fact that it is easy to clean; static electricity can be a problem unless thin metal wires are included in the weave. Polyesters look something like wool but are shinier and less resilient; they produce little static, and can be dyed in brilliant colors.

Along with synthetic fibers have come new manufacturing techniques. Once, all carpets were woven on looms, like fine tapestry. Today, about 95 per cent are tufted, made by machines that sew pile yarn into a backing fabric. The machines produce carpet 25 times faster than the largest looms, at a fraction of the cost.

Because wool and woven carpets are so expensive, the charge for professional installation is a relatively minor part of their total cost. The tufted synthetics, however, are particularly suited to amateur installation. They come in 12-foot rather than the old-style 27-inch widths, so that there are fewer seams to worry about. The seams themselves need no longer be laboriously stitched together—hot-melt seaming tape produces invisible seams in less than 10 minutes. Inexpensive carpeting with padding attached can simply be glued to the floor. Better carpeting requires a separate pad and a slightly more complex installation, but laborsaving devices make the job easy. For example, the paradoxically named tackless strip—a plywood stick bristled with tacks—invisibly holds a carpet to a baseboard, eliminating the visible tacks once used for fastening. These tools and materials have made the traditional carpet craftsman, with a mouthful of tacks and handful of needles and thread, a figure of the past. With reasonable care and clear instructions, you can do the job yourself.

Estimating and Installing Wall-to-wall Carpet

Carpet-laying was once an arcane art performed by veteran craftsmen who invisibly stitched dozens of yards of seams and deftly placed hundreds of hidden tacks to carpet even a small room. Today special tools and materials—tackless strip (*page 100*), heat-sealing seaming tape (*page 105*) and the power stretcher and knee-kicker (*pages 106 and 107*)—have so simplified the job that it can be done by an amateur. Two methods are used, since there are two types of carpet: conventional (*pages 100-109*), which must be laid over separate padding, and cushion-back (*pages 100-111*), which has a layer of foam padding bonded to its back.

Some conventional carpets are still made in the traditional way: the pile—the fibers that constitute the cushiony surface—is woven as part of a backing of tough, open-weave jute-and-cotton threads that give a carpet its horizontal strength. Such carpets as Axminster or Wilton require special installation techniques that are best left to professionals. These kinds of carpets are so expensive that the cost of having them professionally installed—a per square yard charge, regardless of the price of the carpet—is proportionately small.

Most carpets are tufted: that is, their pile—whether made of wool or any of several synthetics—is machine-stitched into a backing that is made beforehand. They may be made with loop pile or cut pile (*bottom, right*), a distinction that is important to the techniques used when cutting carpet to fit your room (*page 103*). Sculptured carpets are made with both loop and cut pile.

When newly manufactured carpet is rolled up as it comes off the machine, the pile fibers are pressed down in the same direction, never to return to their original position. This "pile direction" affects appearance and installation technique.

You can tell pile direction by stroking it: stroking against the pile direction will raise the nap. When you "look into" the pile, with the fibers leaning toward you, a carpet takes on its deepest hue. When you are "looking over" the pile, the carpet appears flatter and lighter in color. If possible, carpet should be installed with the pile leaning toward the main entrance to the room, presenting its fullest, richest appearance. To help hide the seam where two pieces of carpet are joined, the pile of at least one side should lean over the seam. In a doorway connecting two rooms, the pile from both sides may lean over the seam, but within a room the pile of every section of carpet must lean the same way or the pieces will show up as different hues.

Pile direction is one of several factors that must be taken into account when you are planning the layout of a carpet in a room and calculating how much to buy. Some others to remember are:

☐ Never run a seam into a doorway. The foot traffic thus directed along the seam length may loosen it.

☐ Run the longest seam in the room toward the major light source—usually the largest window. A seam running parallel to light rays is much less apparent than one running across them.

☐ Keep seams away from high traffic areas, such as between doors of a room.

☐ The best way to determine how much carpet you will need is to make a scale drawing of the area to be carpeted on graph paper. Choose a scale that will keep the drawing a convenient size; equating each square of the graph paper to a square foot usually works well.

☐ Make separate measurements of the entire length of each wall and then the shorter distances between its various features, such as doorjambs. Double-check for error by making sure the sum of the parts is equal to the whole. Compare diagonal measurements and the distances between walls to see if the walls are skewed or bowed. Plot the walls, doors and windows on the graph paper.

☐ Include the areas where the carpet will extend into doorways or bays as part of the room's overall dimensions. Add 3 inches to both the length and the width of the floor to allow for error and the final trimming of the carpet.

Now, bearing in mind the rules about pile direction and location of seams, figure out how many running yards of carpet 12 feet wide you need for the room, trying to keep the number of seams and the amount of wasted carpet to a minimum. Experiment by cutting to scale a piece of graph paper representing a length of carpet 12 feet wide and testing how it can be divided to cover the floor.

If the carpet is patterned, you must take into account the repeat—the distance from the point where a pattern begins to where it begins again—in order to be sure of matching the pattern along a seam. If your scheme involves matching the pattern only lengthwise across two original edges of the carpet (*opposite, center*), simply allow for a full extra repeat on one of the lengths, and you will be able to adjust it to match. Take your scale drawing to your carpet dealer and ask him to check your estimates.

Your scale drawing will tell you also how much padding and tackless strip is required. Since padding, which comes in rolls 4½ to 12 feet wide, can be cut into pieces of varying size and put down in crazy-quilt fashion, compute the square footage of the room and buy just a little more than is necessary to cover that area. Determine the type of tackless strip needed (*page 100*) and buy a few feet more than the perimeter of the area to be carpeted. (If you are replacing a carpet, use the existing tackless strip, as long as both carpets have a similar thickness.)

Before starting, nail uneven boards, remove grilles from heating vents and sweep the floor. Dust can work up through seams in the padding and form streaks in the pile. You may wish to remove shoe moldings (*page 24*); if you do not plan to put them back, repaint the baseboards before laying the carpet.

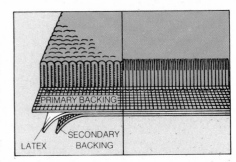

The making of a tufted carpet. The pile yarn of tufted carpet is stitched through a layer of open-weave fabric—the primary backing. A second fabric backing is stuck onto the underside of the first with a coating of latex. When the yarn is left uncut the result is loop-pile tufted carpet (*left*). But the tops of the loops are often split or cut off, making cut-pile tufted carpet (*right*).

Fitting Carpet to the Room

Lengthwise installation. In this typical room, 17 feet by 23 feet, the best plan is lengthwise installation of broadloom 12 feet wide; the rest is filled with two pieces (*1 and 2*) from an extra 4 yards of carpet (*dashed lines, far right*). The major seam will run into the main light source—the window at the left. The pile should lean toward the main door. The large section of full-width carpet will take most of the room's traffic, which passes between the two doors. The seams will be away from heavy traffic and probably partly hidden by furniture. In a smaller room, fill the gap between the main run of carpet and the wall at the top of the drawing with sections so narrow you can cut three or more from the 12-foot broadloom width; if so, you will have to make more seams, but will be paying for less carpet.

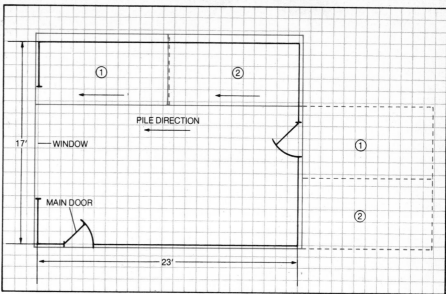

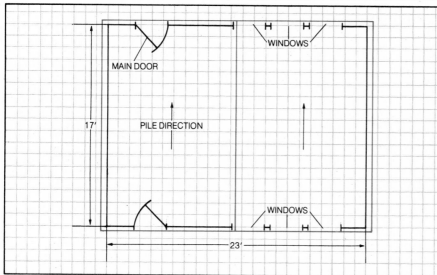

Short sheeting a room. This room, while the same size as that above, has an arrangement of doors and windows that make it preferable to install the length of the carpet across the shorter dimension of the room—a technique called short sheeting. That way, the major seam will be aligned with the light from the windows and will be away from the bulk of traffic that passes between the doors. The pile should lean toward the main door.

Adding a seam to avoid a door. This room is much like that above, center, except that a door is in the middle of one wall and the seam of a normal short sheeting installation would run directly into it, taking the wear of heavy traffic. To avoid this undesirable location of the seam, cut one of the full widths of carpet lengthwise into two pieces and seam them to both sides of the remaining full-width section. The result is two seams instead of one, but neither of them runs directly into a door.

A Foundation of Pads and Pins

Although they will be hidden when the job is finished, tackless strip and padding are essential to the carpeting of a room. The tackless strip is installed around the perimeter of the room to hold the stretched carpet taut *(above, right)*. The padding provides cushioning.

Tackless strip comes in three types. Type C strip, with pins ¼ inch high, is used for thick-yarn shag carpeting. Type D strip has 3/16-inch-high pins suited for carpets having very thin backs. Type E has medium-sized 7/32-inch pins that are right for the great majority of carpets. Place a sample of carpet over a strip and press your fingers into the carpet over the pins, gingerly at first. The carpet and strip are ideally matched if you can discern the tips of the pins without being pricked by them. If you can feel the sharpness of the pins, use strip with shorter pins.

The tackless strip is nailed to most floors but can be glued to tiles. Install it in front of obstacles such as radiators, where you would have difficulty stretching the carpet underneath to the wall. Where carpet will end in a doorway, use special flanged edging *(opposite, center)*.

Padding is made in two basic forms: felt and foam. Good felt padding is made of jute fibers and animal hair pressed together, then coated with latex and imprinted with a waffle-like pattern. It is considered more durable than most foam, a sponge of rubber or synthetic.

While both felt and foam padding are cut and stapled to wood floors similarly *(page 102)*, there are some differences in installation. If a felt padding has a waffle-like imprint on one side, place that side up. On concrete or tile, use linoleum paste to cement down felt padding. When installed, felt padding should be flush with the surrounding tackless strip.

Foam padding that has waffling or fabric on one side is laid with that side up. To affix foam padding to concrete or tile, use adhesive made for that purpose. Seal the seams between sections with duct tape. Bevel the top edges of the padding away from the adjacent tackless strip to prevent the padding—which will probably stretch—from riding up over the tackless strip as the carpet is laid.

Holding carpet without tacks. Tackless strip is made of a three-ply strip of wood 1 inch wide and 9/32 of an inch thick, with sharp pins protruding at a 60° angle from the face to grip the carpet. When the strip is correctly installed, the pins point toward the wall and the printing on the strip can be read from the room. It comes in 4-foot lengths and is fixed to the floor with preset nails. Strip with masonry nails for concrete floors is available. When carpet is stretched over the strip, the pins hold it under tension. The gully formed between the wall and the strip holds the tucked-in edge of the carpet. The strip comes beveled along the wall edge to create a gully if you leave quarter-round shoe moldings in place.

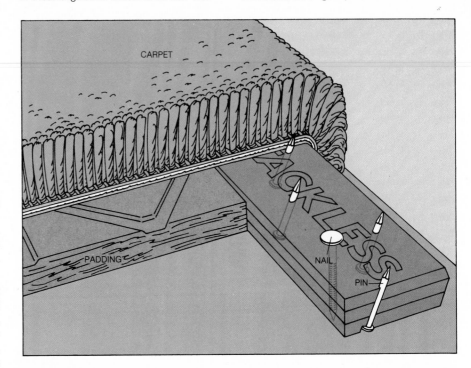

Nailing Tackless Strip in Place

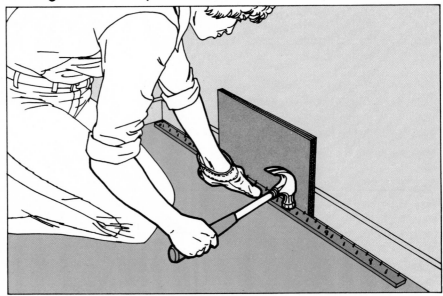

1 **Nailing strips to the floor.** Starting in a corner, hold a piece of strip in a gloved hand and nail it two thirds the thickness of the carpet from the wall—to guide you, use a spacer made by gluing cardboard to the required thickness. If you cannot keep from battering down the carpet-holding pins with the hammer, try a tack hammer, which has a smaller head; however, you will need a 24-ounce hammer when nailing into concrete.

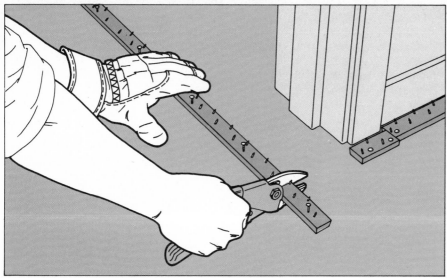

2 Cutting strip. With a saw or garden shears, cut pieces to fit around a doorjamb (*left*) or to fill gaps. If you use shears wear goggles in case the cut piece springs up. Grip the strip in the jaws, position the lower handle against the floor and lean on the upper handle to make the cut. At door openings install small pieces to maintain the correct spacing between the strip and each section of door molding. Drive extra nails so that each piece of strip is held by at least two.

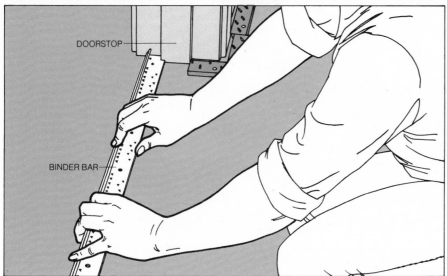

DOORSTOP

BINDER BAR

3 Installing metal strips in doorways. Nail metal edging strip so that its binder bar—the flange that will fold down over the carpet edge—is directly under the door. In doorways where the door opens away from the area to be carpeted, as at left, notch the flat part of the strip to accommodate the doorstop.

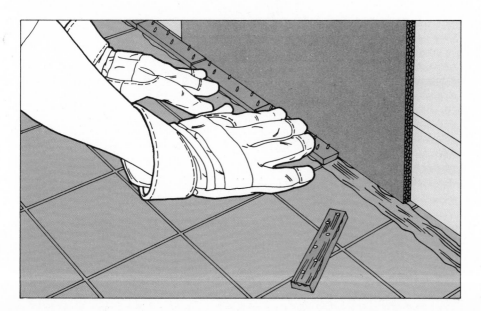

Fastening Strip with Glue

Cementing strip. On an uneven, non-nailable surface such as a tiled floor, cut the strip to the width of each tile—if the tiles are very small, cut the strips about 4 inches long. Clean and sand the surface, then fasten each strip with contact cement. Tap the strip down with a tack hammer. Caution: provide adequate ventilation when using contact cement. Keep the lid on the can when you are not using it. If the cement is flammable, extinguish pilot lights and shut off power to nearby appliances using electric motors.

Laying the Pad

1 **Stapling padding in place.** Cut from the roll of padding a piece large enough to cover one end of the room, slightly overlapping the tackless strip, and staple it into position. Stapling into the depressions of waffled padding, drive the staples at about 6-inch intervals around the edges of the piece. Cut and staple down more padding, butting the pieces together, until the floor is covered.

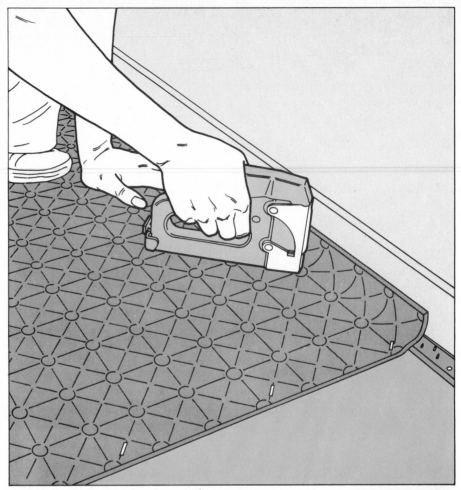

2 **Trimming.** Holding a utility knife at a shallow angle, make a vertical cut along the inside edge of the tackless strip all around the room. For urethane or rubber padding, tilt the knife away from the wall to make a beveled edge so the padding will not ride up over the tackless strip when the carpet is stretched over the strip.

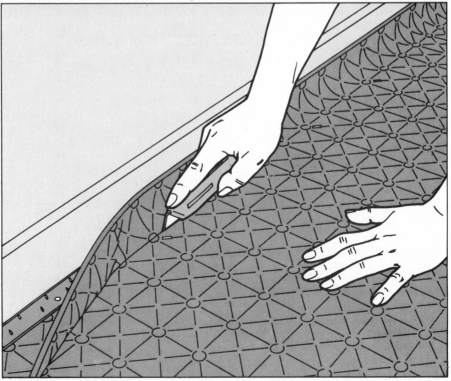

Rough-cutting and Seaming

Now it is time to cut the carpet, according to the scaled plot you made when planning the carpeting of a room *(page 99)*, and roughly position the pieces. Unroll the carpet in an empty room, basement, driveway or yard—over newspaper if necessary—and give it time to flatten.

Cut-pile carpet should be cut from the back *(right)*. Loop-pile should be cut from the front *(below)* to be sure the cut carpet does not remain joined by loops across the cut. When you lay out the pieces in the area to be carpeted, place them so that the pile leans in the same direction. Position the carpet by kicking it *(page 104)*, or by flapping smaller pieces as if shaking a tablecloth, until the excess extends up all walls equally. Make relief cuts at corners *(page 104)*. Hot-melt seaming tape makes joining pieces of carpet easy. But seams across the width of the carpet require special cutting *(page 105)*. In a doorway, make the seam only after the carpet on one side has been stretched and stay-tacked.

If hot-melt carpet seaming tape or the iron that activates it are unavailable, use latex and tape *(page 119)* for the seams.

Two Ways to Cut a Carpet

Cutting a cut-pile carpet. Measure along the face of the unrolled carpet, cut notches in the edges, fold the carpet back and snap a chalk line across it with a string held between the notches. Cut along the chalk line with a knife guided by a good straightedge. Extend the blade of the knife only enough to cut the backing.

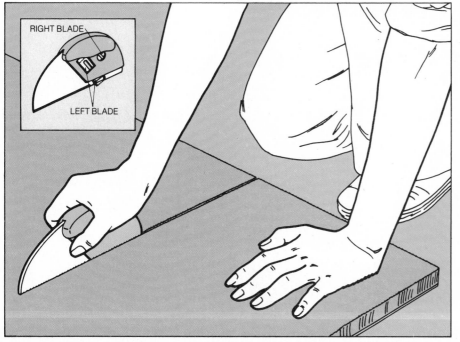

Cutting loop-pile carpet. Measure the carpet and cut it from the face between rows of loops with a row-running "cushion-back" cutter or with a utility knife. If the rows are not straight use a straightedge. If you use the row runner *(inset)*, retract both blades and separate the pile by sliding the runner along the backing. After making a path, extend the blade on the side of the tool next to the section of carpet you will use and make the cut.

Shifting and Snipping to Put a Carpet in Place

1 Kicking carpet into place. When you have placed a cut piece of carpet on the area it will cover, lift a corner, straddle it and kick the carpet with your foot to shift it into position. Caution: do not kick the carpet with your heel—it may tear.

2 Making relief cuts. Where the carpet laps up against a corner that protrudes into a room, cut a vertical slice with a utility knife to allow the carpet on both sides of the corner to lay flat on the floor and lap up neatly along the wall. Cut only into the portion of the carpet that will be trimmed. Make similar cuts at inside corners.

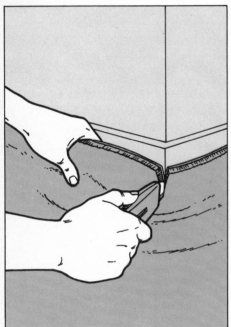

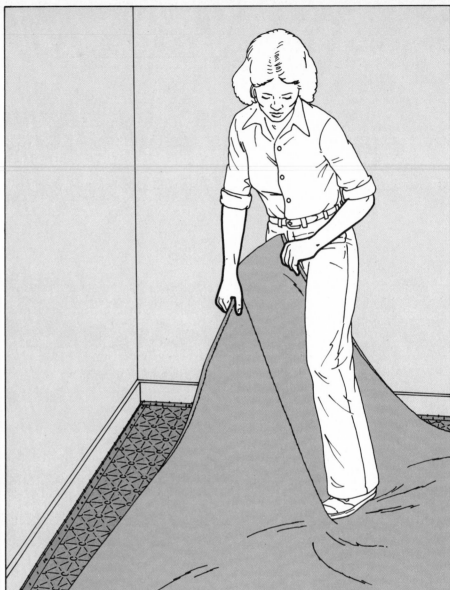

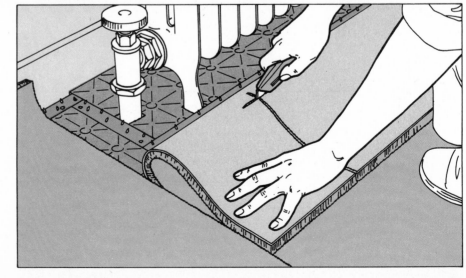

3 Cutting to fit around obstacles. Lap the carpet up against an obstacle, such as the foot of a radiator, fold it back and make a straight cut from there to the carpet's edge; then make a cross-cut just long enough for the carpet to lie roughly flat around the obstacle until you get to final trimming. For a radiator this may involve several cuts out to the edge and several crosscuts to accommodate all the feet and pipes.

Making a Hot-melt Seam

1 **Cutting for a cross seam.** Where you need to make a seam across the breadth of the carpet, overlap the pieces 1 inch, placing on top the piece that has its pile leaning across the join (make sure the edge of this piece is straight). Using the edge of the top piece as a guide, cut the underlying carpet with a row-running knife *(inset)*. Use a utility knife to continue the cuts across the part of the carpet that laps the wall.

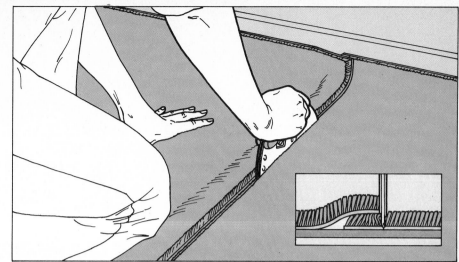

2 **Positioning the tape.** Slip a length of hot-melt seaming tape under one edge of carpet where two butted pieces will be joined. Make sure that the adhesive-coated side faces up. Line up its printed center line with the exposed carpet edge. Warm the seaming iron to 250°—setting number two on some models of irons.

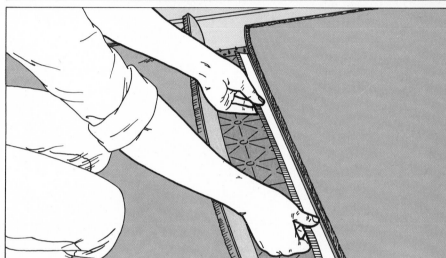

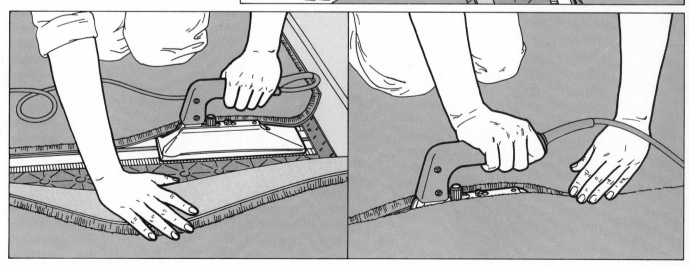

3 **Ironing the tape.** Holding back one side of the carpet, slip the preheated seaming iron onto the tape at one end *(left)*. Center the iron on the tape and let the carpet flop down. Let the iron rest on the tape for 30 seconds. Then draw the iron slowly along the tape for a distance of about 1 foot while you press the carpet down into the adhesive with the other hand *(right)*.

Separate the pile along the seam to check that the backings are butted; if not, force them together with your hands. Place a flat, heavy object—a tray from a tool box or a large book—on top of the seamed carpet. Continue seaming until you get as close as you can to the wall. Wait five minutes for the adhesive to set, then pull the middle of the carpet away from the wall to finish the final few inches at the edge.

Stretching and Fine-Cutting

After you have rough-cut and seamed a carpet, you will need two tools, available at rental agencies, to make it smooth and taut from wall to wall. The first, a knee-kicker, secures an edge of the carpet to the tackless strip and to metal strips across doorways along one wall; the second, called a power stretcher, pulls the carpet across the room and secures it to the strip along the opposite wall.

The knee-kicker has an adjustable gripping head on one end, a cushion for the knee on the other, and an adjustable telescoping handle in between *(inset below)*. When you force the head into the pile at one edge of your carpet, tiny hooks catch the nap and longer teeth reach beneath the pile to the back of the carpet. When you bump the kicking cushion, or pad, with your knee, the knee-kicker shoots forward, carrying the carpet toward the wall; if you have placed the tool in the correct way, the carpet will remain against the wall, caught by the pins in the tackless strip.

When you have secured the carpet at one wall, it can be stretched across the room with a power stretcher, a larger device—as much as 26 feet long when fully extended—with many similarities to the knee-kicker. Besides size, the primary difference between the two tools is that the power stretcher has a lever that extends and locks the tooth-bearing head in place, holding the carpet stretched; it does not rebound as the knee-kicker does. And the lever can be raised or lowered before stretching to adjust the amount of carpet that is pulled. The two tools are used in concert to stretch a carpet in a room *(page 108)*.

After you have the carpet firmly secured all the way around the room, trim the excess and tuck the edge in between the baseboard and the tackless strip. This hides the cut edges of the carpet and locks it to the pins in the strip.

The trimming can be done with a utility knife, but a more precise tool is a wall trimmer, which can be rented. Final finishing includes trimming the carpet around floor duct openings (making sure that grilles cover raw carpet edges) and planing doors so they clear the carpet.

Using a Knee-kicker

Hooking the first edge of the carpet. Place the head of the kicker *(inset)* in the carpet about an inch from the wall, lean on the handle with one hand, and bring your knee smartly against the kicking cushion. The carpet, shoved forward, should catch on the tackless strip, and the excess will lap further up the wall. Before using the kicker, adjust its head until you can feel the teeth on the underside of a scrap of carpet.

As you move along the wall, hold the already secured carpet in place with your free hand so that it does not come unhooked as you kick.

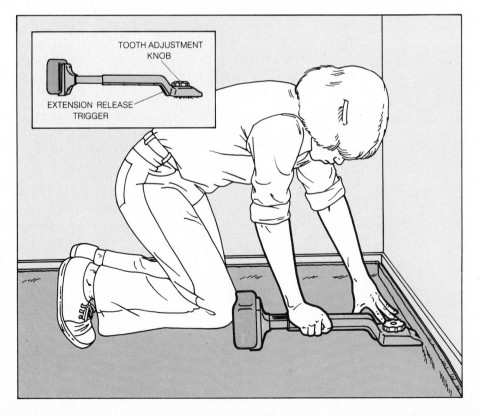

TOOTH ADJUSTMENT KNOB

EXTENSION RELEASE TRIGGER

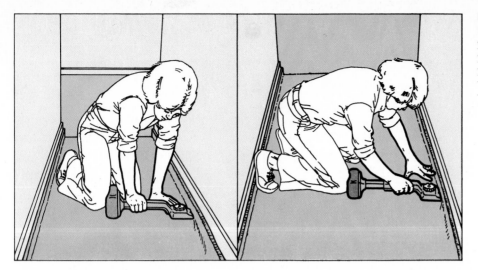

Kicking in narrow places. In restricted spaces like hallways, strike the pad with the side of your knee *(far left)* or adjust the handle so that you can place your foot against the wall and your knee against the kicker pad *(near left)*; then force the kicker to move by pushing against the wall with your foot.

Using a Power Stretcher

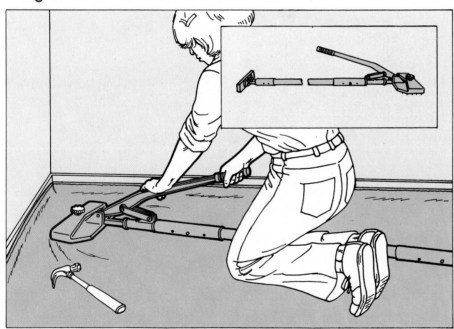

Stretching a carpet. Set the stretcher's teeth for your carpet thickness, adjust its extension tubes so that it reaches from the wall where you secured the carpet with the knee-kicker to a point 6 inches from the opposite wall, and push the lever down—gently, to avoid tearing the carpet—so that the head locks. Use the face of a hammer to iron the carpet firmly onto the tackless strip. If the carpet does not move easily, lift the head, lower the handle to take a smaller bite and try again. To protect the baseboard, place a block of wood wrapped in carpet between it and the tail block of the stretcher.

Ways to get purchase. If there is a doorway in the wall you are stretching from, bridge it with a 2-by-4 *(below, left)*, which will serve as a brace for the tail block. If your room is longer than the maximum length of the stretcher—usually 26 feet—use a 2-by-8 between the tail block and the wall to extend the reach of the device *(below, right)*. Have a helper stand on the board so that it will not slip out of place during the stretch.

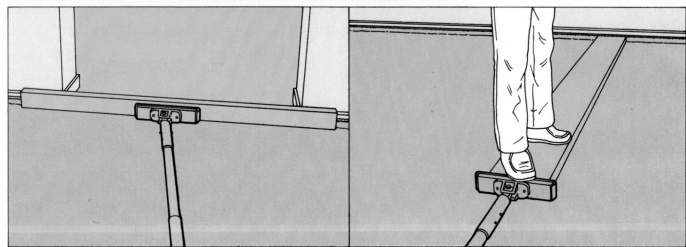

When and Where to Kick and Stretch

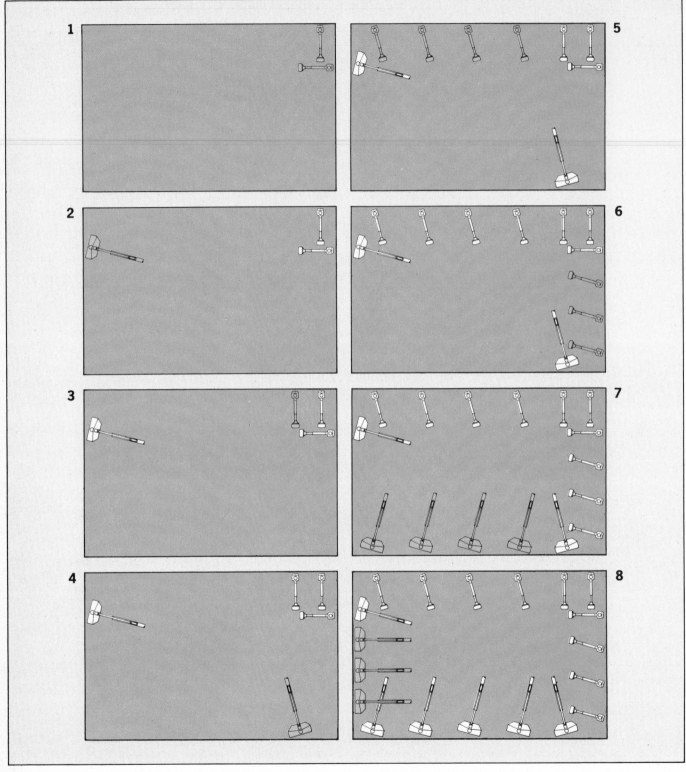

Fitting a taut carpet. These pictures show the sequence in which to use a knee-kicker and a power stretcher to lay a carpet in a typical room. Begin by hooking the carpet in one corner (1) with a knee-kicker and stretch it to an opposite wall with the power stretcher at a slight angle (2). Then secure the carpet against the perpendicular wall next to the same corner (3) with a kicker and stretch it to the opposite wall with the power stretcher (4). Next, hook the carpet with the knee-kicker along the top and right-hand walls (5 and 6) at about a 15° angle and then use the power stretcher along the bottom wall (7) at a similar angle. Finally, stretch from the right-hand wall to the left-hand wall (8).

The Final Trim and Fit

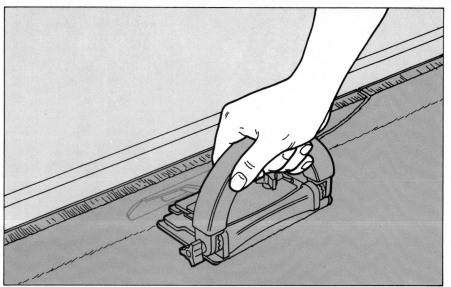

1 **Trimming the carpet.** Adjust a wall trimmer for the thickness of carpet and trim the edges of the carpet all around the room. Start the trimmer in the up-lapping carpet at a 45° angle and level it out when you reach the floor. Trim the last few inches at each end with a utility knife. If you cannot get a wall trimmer, make the final carpet cuts with a utility knife.

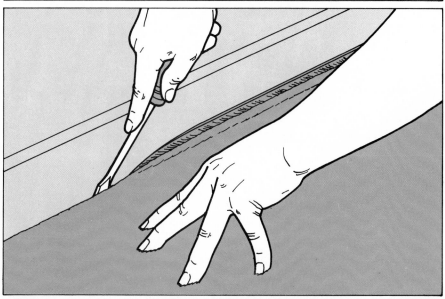

2 **Tucking in the carpet.** Use a screwdriver to tuck the carpet into the gully between the tackless strip and the baseboard. Brush loose strands of yarn out of the gully with the tip of the screwdriver. If the carpet edge bulges too much to tuck in, trim it a bit shorter.

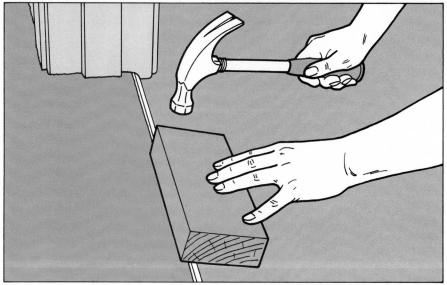

3 **Clamping the carpet at a metal edge.** Trim the carpet to fit under the lip of a metal edge strip; tuck it in and gently tamp the lip down with a hammer and a block of wood. Bend the lip down a little at a time by moving the block of wood along it after each hammer blow.

Cushion-back: Easy to Install

Cushion-back carpet—carpet bonded to its own padding, generally dense foam rubber—is the easiest kind to install. It requires no stretching, no specialized tools and no tackless strips. It is simply cemented down—or, in some cases, stuck to the floor with double-faced tape *(right)*. Also, cushion-back carpet is usually less expensive than carpet installed over separate padding.

Cushion-back, however, does have disadvantages. Although it goes down easily, once cemented it is impossible to remove intact—the cushion-backing rips off the face of the carpet as it is pulled up. The carpet cannot be used again and the backing and adhesive must be scraped off the floor. And the foam backing of some cheap cushion-back carpets may decompose in a few years. Heavier backing generally lasts longer. Although weight is not the only determinant of carpet life, 36 ounces per square yard is the recommended minimum.

For cementing down most cushion-back carpets, use the kind of latex adhesive sold for use on sheet flooring, such as linoleum. Carpets with vinyl backing, or those to be used below ground level, however, require a special adhesive; follow the carpetmaker's recommendation.

Before laying the carpet, remove all dust, wax and paint from the floor, patch cracks and secure loose tiles or floorboards. The floor must be dry. A remedy for occasional moisture in a concrete floor is a layer of concrete sealer. However, if water rising from the ground leaves the floor permanently damp, it is best to forgo carpeting entirely, as the moisture will rot the cushion-back. Test for water seepage with a sheet of plastic taped to the floor *(page 38)*. At doorways, install flanged metal edging similar to the kind used for conventional carpet *(page 101)*, but without teeth.

Many floors are so large that carpet cannot be laid without a seam. In such cases, begin to cement under the seam area *(Step 1)*. If the room needs only one piece, lay the carpet out, fold it in half with the triangular folds described in Step 4 and proceed with installation according to that and subsequent steps.

1 Preparing to make a seam. Before applying adhesive *(below)*, rough-cut and lay out the carpet as you would a conventional carpet *(pages 103-104)*, except that you should always cut cushion-back from the face. Snap a chalk line on the floor where the seam will run. Align the edge of one piece of carpet with the line and pull the other piece so that its edge overlaps the first by ¼ inch. Fold both pieces back about 3 feet. With a ³⁄₃₂-inch notched trowel, spread a thin, even layer of adhesive on the exposed floor. Roll one piece of carpet onto the adhesive, lining it up with the chalk mark. Working from there toward the wall, use your hands to rub out any air bubbles trapped beneath the carpet.

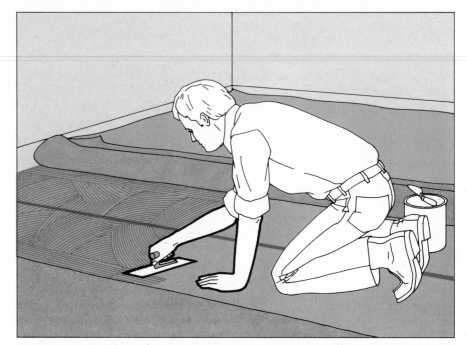

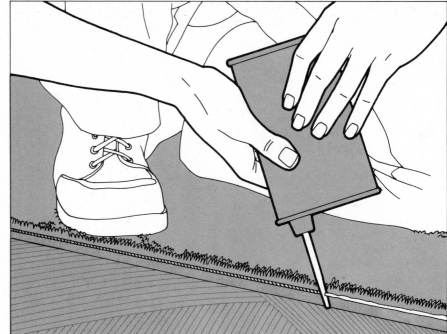

2 Gluing the seam. Apply a bead of seam adhesive *(above)* to the primary backing—just between the pile and the cushion—at the edge of the cemented-down piece of carpet. Work carefully to avoid getting any excess adhesive on the pile of the carpet. To make the job easy and accurate, notch the nozzle of the applicator at the height of the primary backing, and then run the tip along the floor while the adhesive feeds onto the carpet edge.

3 Making a compression seam. Unfold the second piece of carpet and position it on the floor. Butt the edge of this piece of carpet against that of the glued-down piece and work any bulges resulting from the overlap away from the seam with your fingers until you reach the unglued area. When gaps occur at the seam, seal them by pulling and pressing the carpet edges together with your fingers until the two pieces meet all along the seam.

4 Completing the cementing. Fold one piece of carpet back from the wall until you reach the part that has already been cemented to the floor. To prevent the carpet from grabbing along the wall as you fold it back, first fold each corner of the carpet at a 45° angle toward the center of the seam. Trowel the adhesive onto the exposed floor and unfold the carpet in reverse order, rubbing any wrinkles or ridges out toward the wall with your hands or with the paper core of a

carpet roll. Repeat this process on the other side of the room. When the carpet is cemented down, crease it along the walls with a screwdriver or stair tool *(page 114)*.

Trim off excess at a distance above the floor equal to the thickness of the carpet. Then tuck the edge of the carpet against the wall with the screwdriver or stair tool. Tamp down the flanges of the doorway edgings.

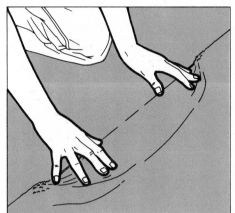

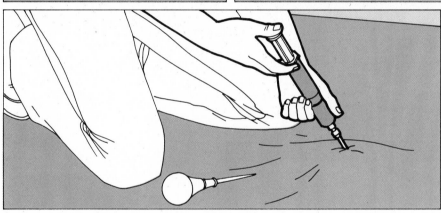

5 Flattening a bubble. Where the carpet is not adhering to the floor, poke an awl through it and use a plastic syringe—which can be bought from a carpet-supply dealer—to inject a special quick-drying cement called contact adhesive into the hole. Then press down on the carpet with your hands until it holds firmly to the floor.

Easier Yet—Taped Cushion-back

Short of just letting the carpet lie loose on the floor, no installation could be easier than sticking down cushion-back with double-faced tape. Unfortunately, the results are rarely satisfying. The carpet will develop wrinkles between the strips of tape and is likely to come unstuck altogether if it gets much wear. But it does provide a simple, quick and cheap way to carpet an area where permanence is unimportant.

In a lightly traveled room, you need to apply tape only around the perimeter, flush with the walls, with a double strip of tape in front of any doorways. In

a busier room, lay tape not only around the perimeter, but also diagonally 1 foot apart across the floor.

Stick down the tape, folding under a corner of each strip to provide a tab for removing the paper covering the face of the tape. Position the rough-cut carpet on the floor and fold back one side in the triangular manner described in Step 4 above. Peel the protective cover from the strips of tape and roll the carpet onto the taped area. Then press the carpet onto the tape with your fingers. Finish the job by trimming the carpet along the walls.

The Right Way to Lay Carpet on a Stairway

A stairway is no place to economize on carpeting; it gets too much wear, especially at the nosing of the treads. The nap of a cheap carpet with a low pile density will soon wear away there, exposing the carpet backing in an effect that carpet men call "grinning."

The padding beneath a stair carpet must be stong enough to absorb the shock of heavy footfalls. Many professionals believe the best padding is a high-quality urethane, which can cost as much yard for yard as the carpet. In most installations a dense felt padding will be almost as effective and much less costly.

Because footsteps, whether ascending or descending, exert pressure toward the nosing, the pile of the carpet should also run down the stairs, toward the nosing, so that it yields to foot pressure instead of resisting it. (If the pile leans toward the top of the stairs, carpet life may be reduced by as much as half.)

When estimating the amount of carpet needed for a stairway, begin by establishing the breadth of carpeting for a straight flight. Carpeting is usually laid wall to wall on closed stairways or from a wall to the base of the balusters on stairways with an open side. The edges of the carpet must roll under about 1¼ inches; therefore, add 2½ inches to the width measurement. To allow for the pile of carpet that extends to all the sides from the roll-under, deduct twice the height of the pile. The result is the breadth of carpet that is needed.

If the stairway carpet is part of an installation that includes a room or a hallway, you may be able to plan your carpet cuts to cover the stairway in one continuous length. When you carpet only the stairway, however, you probably will have to cover it in sections cut from broadloom carpet. If your final figure for the width of the carpet needed is 36 inches or less, you can get four pieces from a standard roll of broadloom, which is 12 feet wide; if the figure is more than 36 inches, you will get only three pieces from a standard roll.

To estimate the number of running yards of broadloom carpet needed for the straight flights of your stairs, determine the length of the stairway to be covered *(Step 1)* and divide by the number of widths you can obtain. This is only a rough estimation; the final figure may be somewhat higher, because two separate lengths of carpet must always meet at a tread-riser crotch. Each piece, therefore, must run from an upper end at the back of a tread to a lower end at the bottom of a riser. Check your sections for this fit and add additional length if necessary. When you begin cutting the carpet—and the padding—use the method appropriate to its type *(pages 102-103)*.

A landing carpet is measured, cut and installed in the same way as floor carpet, but it must also cover the first riser down from the landing. Fasten the riser portion at the bottom of the riser before stretching the carpet over the landing.

When a stairway winds around a corner, the best way to determine the amount of carpet you will need for its wedge-shaped steps, called winder steps, is to cut paper templates. Each winder step will be carpeted separately and each template should cover one tread and the riser underneath it. Add an additional inch to the depth of a template to allow for the bulge of padding over the nosing of the treads, and on an open side, allow for a 1¼-inch roll-under.

When cutting the carpet for a winder step, set the template so its bottom edge aligns with the weft, or cross threads, of the carpet. The warp, or lengthwise threads, will run vertically up the riser and break squarely over the nosing, making the carpet less vulnerable to wear. When installing the piece, attach it to the tackless strip on the riser; stretch it over the tread. A closed side of a winder tread is carpeted like a landing on tackless strip. If the wall has a pronounced curve, cut the tackless strip into small pieces that follow the arc. On an open side, roll the carpet edge under and tack it into place at the back of the tread.

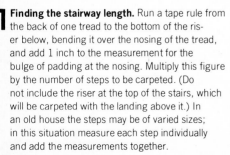

1 **Finding the stairway length.** Run a tape rule from the back of one tread to the bottom of the riser below, bending it over the nosing of the tread, and add 1 inch to the measurement for the bulge of padding at the nosing. Multiply this figure by the number of steps to be carpeted. (Do not include the riser at the top of the stairs, which will be carpeted with the landing above it.) In an old house the steps may be of varied sizes; in this situation measure each step individually and add the measurements together.

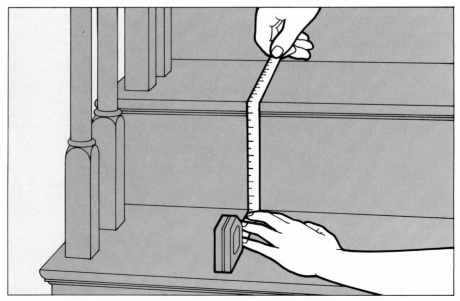

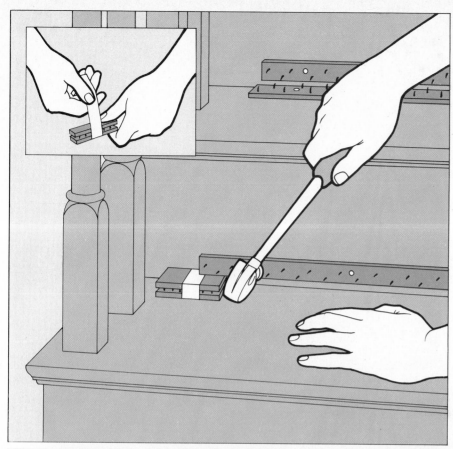

2 **Installing the strip.** Cut a tackless strip *(page 101, Step 2)* 2½ inches shorter than the width of a step and nail the strip to the riser with its pins pointing down. To position the strip at the correct distance above the tread, rest it on spacers made by pulling the nails from short pieces of tackless strip and taping the strips together, pins to pins *(inset)*. Nail tackless strip of the same length to the tread ⅝ inch from the riser, with the pins of this strip pointing toward the riser. Repeat the process for each riser and tread.

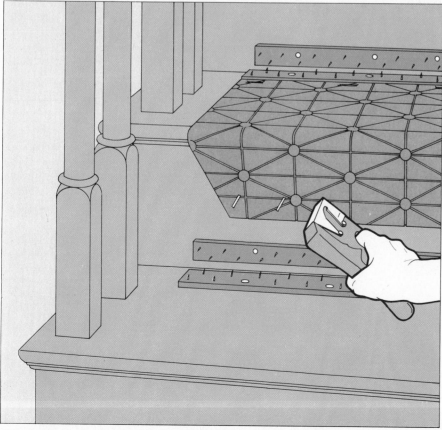

3 **Installing the padding.** Cut a piece of padding 2½ inches shorter than the width of a step, butt it flush to the tackless strip and staple it onto the tread; then pull it over the nose of the step and staple it about 2 or 3 inches down the riser. If one side of the stairway is open, cut the riser portion of the padding away from the nosing at an angle on the open side so that it will not be seen when carpeting is installed.

4 Rolling the edges. Lay the carpet face down, snap chalk lines 1¼ inches from each side to mark the crease of the roll-under, and score the back of the carpet along the chalked lines with an awl. As you score the lines fold the carpet edges over with your fingers. Then position the carpet roughly on the stairway. Caution: be sure that the pile leans down the stairs.

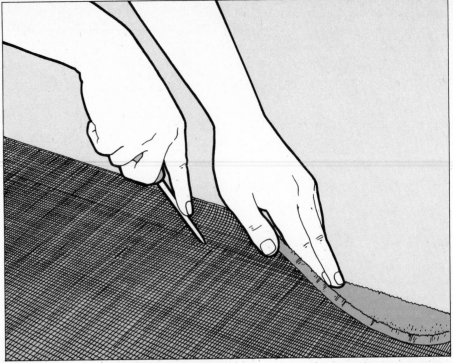

5 Securing the bottom edge. Pull the edge of the carpet down over the tackless strip on the bottom riser with an awl until about ⅜ inch laps onto the floor, and press the carpet onto the pins with your fingers. Iron the carpet along the strip with the head of a carpet hammer to tuck the excess into the gully between the tackless strip and floor. Secure the rolled-under edges with a 24-ounce carpet tack driven through the carpet and into the bottom of the riser on each side.

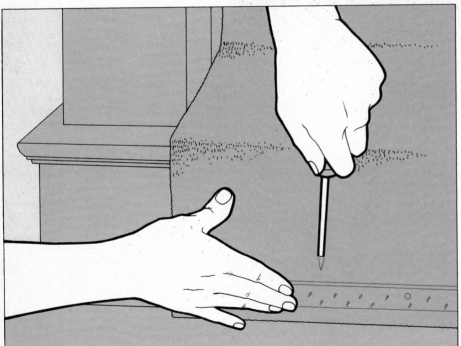

STAIR TOOL

6 Covering the tread. Stretch the carpet over the bottom tread with a knee-kicker and, at the same time, push it into the space behind the tackless strip with a stair tool; the pins of the tackless strip at the back of the tread should grip and hold the carpet backing. Begin this step of the job at the center of the tread and stretch the carpet directly back toward the stair riser; then work the carpet outward toward the edges of the stair tread. For this part of the job, angle the knee-kicker away from the center.

7 **Adjusting the width.** If the width of a tread varies from front to back, push an awl through the top layer of the carpet's rolled-under edge, pierce the lower layer with the tip and, using the awl like a lever, shift the rolled-under edge to make the carpet fit the width at every point.

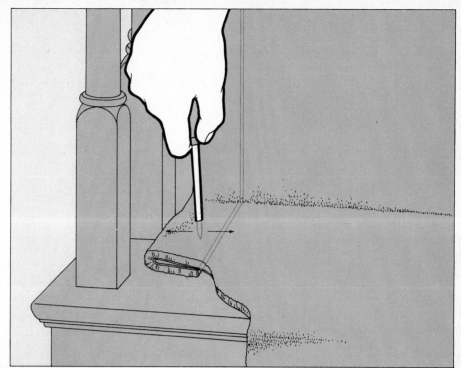

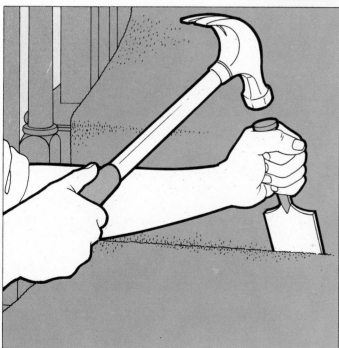

8 **Forcing the carpet into the crotch.** Using a stair tool and a hammer, drive the carpet into the space between the tackless strips on the tread and riser along the full length of the tread-riser crotch. By doing this, you will tighten the carpet over the tread and also fix the carpet to the tackless strip on the riser.

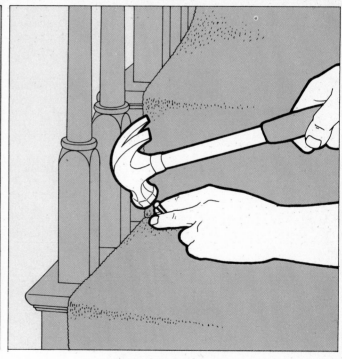

9 **Tacking at the crotch.** Secure the rolled edges at the tread-riser crotch with 24-ounce carpet tacks driven through the carpet and into the crotch at each side.

You are now ready to stretch the carpet on the treads above. When you reach the end of a length of carpet, drive a tack through each rolled-under edge into the back of the tread, trim off any excess carpet with a utility knife and fit the next piece to the next riser (*Step 5*).

Unseen Repairs for Unsightly Stains and Tears

The most carefully tended carpets can suffer accidental damage. The flick of a cigarette or a fragment popped from the log of a fireplace can cause small but noticeable burns. The sharp edge of a child's broken toy cuts a swath through the pile of a carpet or rips the backing underneath. And stains from some spilled liquids stubbornly resist detergents and spot removers. But with a few scraps of matching carpet and some inexpensive tools and materials, you can make durable, almost invisible repairs.

Set scraps aside when the carpet is laid or ask for some from the seller when you buy a carpeted house. If no scraps have been saved, take them from unseen areas such as within closets.

Many jobs call for a tuft-setter, which is a special tool for fixing tufts of pile in place. If you cannot find a tuft-setter at a hardware store or carpet supplier, you can make your own *(below)*. Depending on the task, you also may need such items as carpet-seam tape, latex seam adhesive in a plastic squeeze bottle and the carpet layer's indispensable aid, a knee-kicker *(page 106)*.

Before you begin to repair a damaged carpet, familiarize yourself with its special characteristics. Loop pile, for example, requires techniques different from those used on cut pile, and carpeting that is installed over padding is handled differently from carpeting that is bonded to a foam backing.

Although most carpet repairs are not difficult, they demand patience. When you replace tufts, for example, do not hurry the work; the best results will come from building up the pile over the damaged area carefully, one tuft at a time. Apply latex adhesive sparingly, so that no excess oozes onto the surface of the carpet. Before you cut a patch, make sure it will match the pattern and the tilt of the pile in the area that is damaged.

You should always use the smallest piece of scrap carpet first, so that if you make an error, there will be larger scraps available to correct it. And when you embark upon a job that is new to you, take the time to practice on unneeded scraps of carpet before tackling the real thing.

A Tool for Setting Carpet Tufts

A device for implanting new pile, called a tuft-setter, can be purchased, but you can make one yourself from a large needle—the type used for sewing squares of knitting together—and a ⅜-inch wood dowel. Cut a 4-inch length from the dowel and drill a 1/16-inch hole about 1 inch deep into its end. Insert the needle point into the hole and tap the other end of the needle with a hammer, driving the point into the wood. Using wire cutters or the cutting section of a pair of long-nose pliers, clip most of the eye from the needle, leaving a shallow V-shaped end *(inset)*. To complete the tuft-setter, round and smooth this end with a small file or sharpening stone.

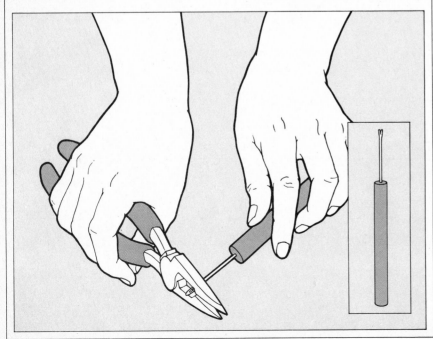

Restoring a Small Area

1 **Removing the pile.** Using scissors with short, curved blades—a pair of ordinary cuticle scissors will do—cut the damaged pile down to the carpet backing, then pick out the stubs of the tufts or loops with tweezers. For replacement pile, pick tufts or unravel lengths of looped yarn from the edge of a carpet scrap.

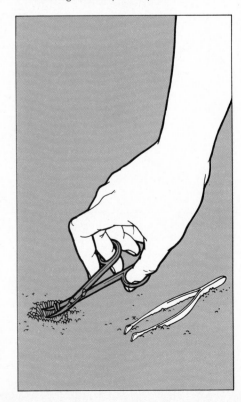

2 **Applying adhesive.** Squeeze a little latex cement onto a carpet scrap, dip a cotton-tipped swab into the cement and lay a spot of the adhesive at the point where you will begin setting new tufts or loops. The cement dries rapidly—apply it to one small area at a time.

3 **Replacing the pile.** For a cut-pile carpet, fold a tuft into a V over the tip of the tuft-setter and punch it into the latex-swabbed carpet backing with one or two light taps of a hammer. Repeat the process, setting the tufts close together and spreading more adhesive as it is needed. Do not drive the tufts so deep that the replacement pile is lower than that of the surrounding carpet; to get the best results, set the new pile high and trim it even.

For a carpet with loop pile *(inset)*, punch one end of a long piece of yarn into the backing with a tuft-setter, then form successive loops from the same piece and set the bottom of each loop. Check each loop to be sure that it is the same height as the existing pile. Pull a short loop up from the backing with tweezers; punch a long one farther into the backing with the tuft-setter.

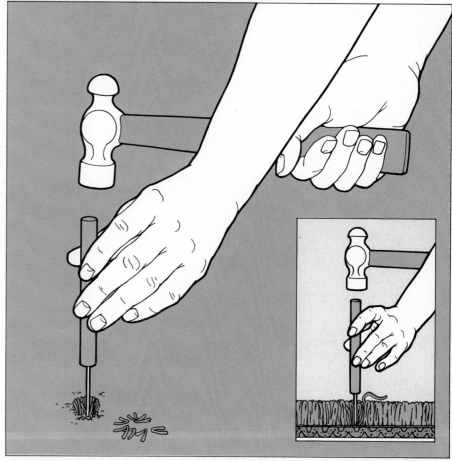

Patching a Large Area

1 **Stay-tacking.** To reduce the tension of the carpet over the area to be patched, set the teeth of a knee-kicker (*page 106*) about a foot from the area and push the kicker forward. Be careful not to push so hard you raise a hump in the carpet. Lay a strip of carpet upside down just ahead of the knee-kicker and tack the strip into the floor at 3- to 4-inch intervals. Release the knee-kicker and repeat the process, called stay-tacking, on the other three sides of the area.

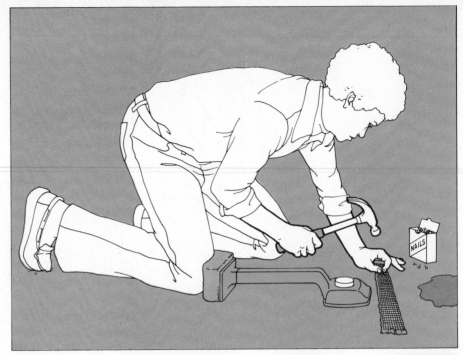

2 **Cutting a patch.** From scrap that matches the carpet, cut a patch slightly larger than the damaged area. To avoid damaging the pile at the edges of the patch while cutting, open a pathway through the tufts or loops with a blunt tool, such as a Phillips screwdriver, then pull the pile away from the cutting line with your fingers as you make the cut.

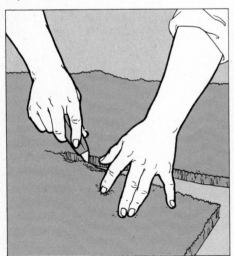

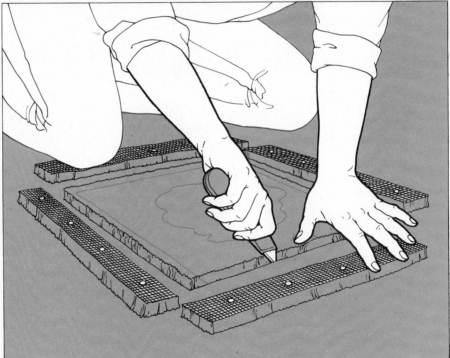

3 **Cutting a hole.** Place the patch over the damaged area, matching both pattern and pile direction, and, using one edge of the patch as a guide, cut through the carpet and its backing to points about ½ inch from the patch corners. Open a pathway for the knife between rows of pile as you cut, and do not cut the pad beneath the carpet. Lift the other three edges of the patch and cut completely around the damaged area, making a hole about ½ inch smaller than the patch. Discard the section you have cut out.

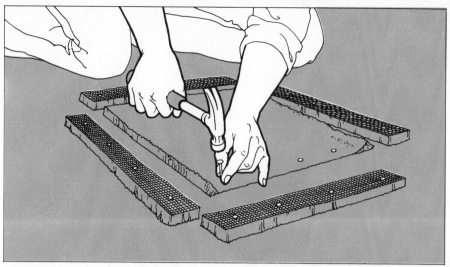

4 **Trimming the hole.** Return the patch to its original position and stay-tack the edge used as a guide for the first carpet cut; the patch should overlap three sides of the hole you have made in the carpet. Using the anchored patch as a template, cut the carpet to fit snugly around all sides of the patch. Pull the stay tacks from the patch and remove the patch from the hole.

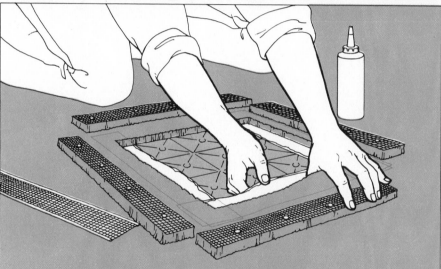

5 **Placing the seam tape.** The patch will be held by seam tape slipped partway under the carpet. Cut four strips of seam tape about an inch longer than the sides of the hole and coat the strips with thin layers of latex seam adhesive—just enough to fill in the weave of the tape. Slip the strips beneath the edges of the hole so that a cut edge of the carpet lies over the center line of each strip. Squeeze a thin bead of adhesive along the edges of the carpet backing, but avoid getting any adhesive on the pile.

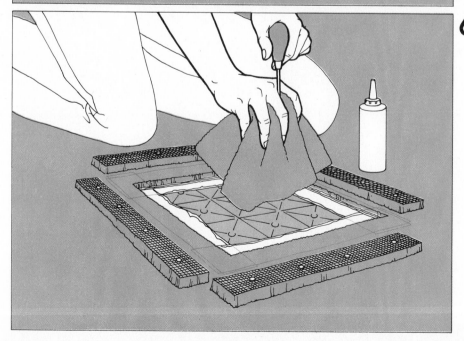

6 **Putting in the patch.** Push a thin awl down through the center of the patch and cup your other hand over the patch so that its sides are folded downward into a tent shape. Position the patch over the hole—check to be sure that it matches the carpet in pattern and pile direction—and push it down off the awl and into the hole. As the edges of the patch move outward, they should pick up small amounts of adhesive from the tape. Push the edges of patch and carpet together with your finger tips and press on the seam around the patch with the heels of your hands. Use the awl to free tufts or loops of pile crushed into the seam, and brush your fingers back and forth across the seam to blend the pile of carpet and patch.

After about five hours, pull out the stay tacks around the patch and restore the overall tension on the carpet with the knee-kicker.

Mending a Surface Rip

1 Cementing the area. If the backing is undamaged, lift the torn section of carpet face
away from it, clean out any loose pile or dried cement and apply latex seam adhesive to the
backing. Smear the adhesive into a light film over
all of the exposed backing.

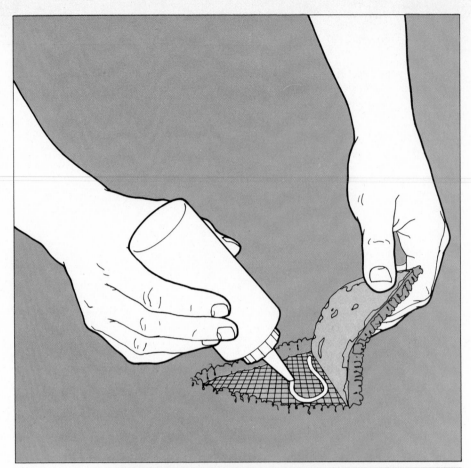

2 Closing the rip. Push the edges of the rip together and hold them in place with one hand while
you rub the carpet surface with a smooth object,
such as the bottom of a soft-drink bottle. Rub
firmly from the rip toward the sound carpet to
work the adhesive well into the fibers of the
backing without forcing it out of the rip. If any adhesive does ooze up to the surface, clean it off
immediately with water and detergent. After four
or five hours, when the adhesive has dried, replace any missing pile (*pages 116-117*).

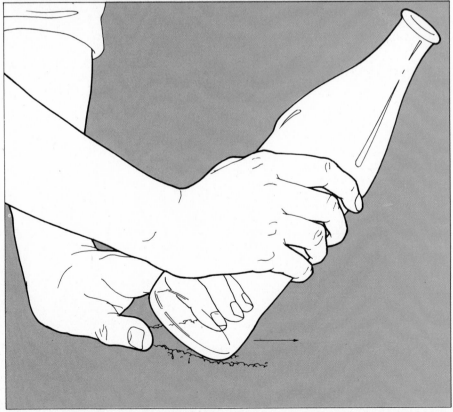

Stitching Through the Carpet Backing

1 Turning back the carpet. If the rip goes through the backing, reduce the tension of the carpet at the corner of the room closest to the rip, using a knee-kicker *(page 106)*; then lift the carpet from the hooks of the tackless strip with an awl. When the corner is free pull the carpet from the strip with your hands along the two walls. Free the carpet along the adjoining walls until you can turn it back to expose the rip in the backing.

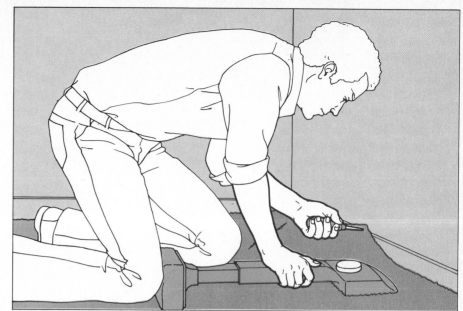

2 Sewing the rip. Using a heavy needle and carpet thread that matches the color of the pile, mend the rip with stitches about an inch long and ¼ inch apart; pull each stitch tight before starting the next. If the angle of the rip permits, run the stitches parallel to the rows of carpet pile; otherwise, sew at right angles to the rows of pile. Under the turned backing, run the needle through—not over—the pile; check the face of the carpet frequently to be sure the stitches are concealed. When the entire rip has been sewn, knot the thread around the last stitch.

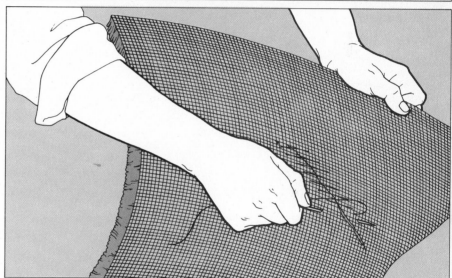

3 Sealing the seam. Apply a wavy bead of latex adhesive over the sewn seam and spread it with a scrap of carpet, rubbing it into the backing and stitches. Cover the wet latex with facial tissue to protect the pad, then turn the carpet back into place and reattach it to the tackless strips *(pages 106-107)*. After the carpet is reinstalled, replace any damaged pile *(pages 116-117)*.

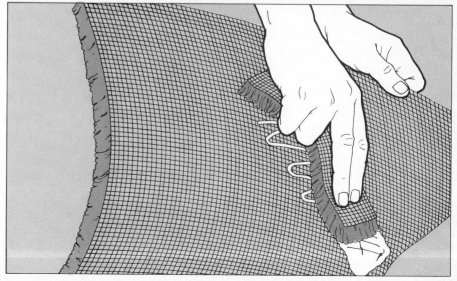

Repairs for Cushion-back

Only one repair job—replacing pile with a tuft-setter in a small damaged area *(page 116)*—is exactly the same for both cushion-back and conventional carpets. Otherwise, the differences between the two types of carpet call for different methods of repair. Cushion-back is usually glued to the floor and cannot be turned back from a corner to sew up a rip. Even when the carpet is installed with double-faced tape rather than glue, its single layer of woven backing (conventional carpet has two layers) normally is not strong enough to hold stitches. Rips, like large damaged areas, must be repaired by patching.

Since cushion-back carpet is not installed under tension, no knee-kicking or stay-tacking is necessary before patching. Cushion-back carpet has one other important difference from conventional: while pile rows run straight along its length as on a conventional carpet, the intersecting rows of pile may not run straight across its width—instead of meeting the longitudinal rows at a 90° angle, the intersecting rows may lie along a diagonal. When you cut a patch, run the tip of a Phillips screwdriver along the crosswise rows at various angles until you can easily clear pathways for your utility knife. The resulting shape may be a skewed parallelogram instead of a rectangle. Cut out the damaged area to fit the patch as you would on conventional carpet *(page 118)*, slicing through the cushion-back all the way to the floor.

When the carpet has no pattern, it is simpler to cut the patch and hole with a special tool called a circle cutter *(top right)*. A circle cutter will slice through the loops or tufts, making the mend more visible. But you may still prefer to use this tool for a quick and easy job. Whichever cutting method you use, the patch must be cemented to both the floor and the surrounding carpet *(right)*.

1 Using a circle cutter. With the blade adjusted for the thickness of the carpet and the shaft extended and locked in a radius that will take in the whole area of damage, set the center pin of the circle cutter into the middle of the damaged spot, press down on the head and rotate the tool clockwise. Turn the head repeatedly in complete circles until the blade has cut through both the woven backing and the foam cushion. Maintaining the same blade and shaft settings, repeat the process to cut a patch from a scrap of matching carpet.

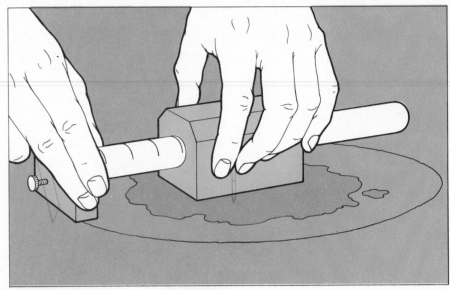

2 Applying floor adhesive. Scrape any dried cement from the hole in the carpet with a sharpened putty knife and, using a ³⁄₃₂-inch notched trowel, spread on multipurpose flooring adhesive. The adhesive should lie on the floor in grooves; to be sure that it does, press down on the trowel hard enough to remove all the adhesive from between notches.

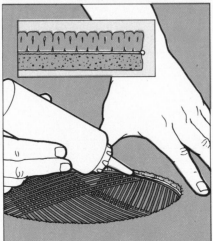

3 Applying seam adhesive. Squeeze a thin bead of cushion-back seam adhesive along the edge of the woven carpet backing inside the hole. Caution: the bead should cover only the woven backing *(inset)*; avoid getting adhesive on the pile or the foam cushion.

Set the patch in the hole as you would when patching conventional carpet *(page 119, Step 6)*. If the patch is small enough to cup in your hand, you need not use an awl.

Keeping Carpets Spotless

Routine carpet care requires common-sense procedures. Using a vacuum cleaner once a week, with a touch-up in between on paths of heavily trafficked areas, diminishes the danger that abrasive, tracked-in grit will cut the fibers. The occasional rearrangement of the furniture reduces wear on specific areas. To avoid sun bleaching, draw the blinds. Once a year or so, shampoo or steam clean the carpet *(pages 124-125)*.

But routine means will not do when you confront that perennial household emergency, the spilling of substances that can leave stains. Clean up promptly; even if the spill does not seem sticky, walking on it will probably darken the stain. After picking up solids with a spatula or dull knife, consult the chart at the right for the correct cleaning agents and techniques for more than three dozen common staining substances.

Finding the right treatment. In the alphabetized column at the left of this chart, find the material that has stained your carpet and treat it by the method given in the right-hand column. You may have to apply several cleaning solutions in succession. One is a standard commercial dry-cleaning fluid such as trichloroethane; do not use carbon tetrachloride, gasoline or lighter fluid. Mix the following three solutions yourself, according to these recipes:
□ Shampoo: one teaspoon of carpet shampoo in one cup of water.
□ Vinegar: one-third cup of white vinegar and two-thirds cup of water.
□ Ammonia: one tablespoon of clear household ammonia in one-half cup of water.

Do not pour any stain remover directly onto a carpet; instead, wet a pad in the solution, blot the stain and work from the edge to the center with a circular or twisting motion. Always follow a shampoo solution by sponging with water. Cover the spot with a pad of paper towels weighted by a book and left five or six hours.

Removing nail polish, furniture stain, household cement, dried paint or large quantities of oil, paint or ink is very difficult. For these stains and for unknown materials that you cannot clean up with shampoo followed by a dry cleaner, call a professional cleaner or repair the carpet by retufting or patching *(pages 116-122)*.

Treatments for Every Stain

Cause of stain	Treatment
Alcoholic beverages	Apply shampoo and vinegar. If traces remain, apply dry cleaner.
Bleach	Apply shampoo and vinegar.
Blood	Sponge with cool water. Apply shampoo, ammonia and vinegar.
Butter, margarine	Apply dry cleaner. If traces remain, apply shampoo.
Candle wax	Apply dry cleaner.
Candy, chocolate	Apply shampoo and vinegar. If traces remain, apply dry cleaner.
Catsup	Apply shampoo.
Chewing gum	Chill with ice cube until gum is brittle. Scrape off with dull knife. Apply dry cleaner.
Coffee, tea	Apply shampoo and vinegar. If traces remain, apply dry cleaner.
Cough syrup	Apply shampoo.
Crayons	Apply dry cleaner and shampoo.
Egg	Apply shampoo, ammonia, vinegar and if traces remain, dry cleaner.
Excrement	Sponge with cool water. Apply shampoo, ammonia and vinegar.
Fruit, fruit juices	Apply shampoo, ammonia, vinegar and if traces remain, dry cleaner.
Furniture polish	Apply dry cleaner and shampoo.
Gravy	Apply shampoo, ammonia, vinegar and if traces remain, dry cleaner.
Grease	Apply dry cleaner.
Ink, washable	Apply shampoo.
Lipstick	Apply dry cleaner, shampoo, ammonia and vinegar.
Milk, ice cream	Apply shampoo, ammonia and vinegar.
Motor oil	Apply dry cleaner, shampoo, ammonia and vinegar.
Mud	Let dry, brush gently, vacuum, then apply shampoo.
Mustard	Apply shampoo and vinegar. If traces remain, apply dry cleaner.
Paint, wet oil-based	Apply dry cleaner.
Paint, wet water-based	Apply shampoo.
Perfume	Apply dry cleaner and shampoo.
Salad dressing	Apply dry cleaner. If traces remain, apply shampoo and vinegar.
Shoe polish	Apply dry cleaner, shampoo, ammonia and vinegar.
Soft drinks	Apply shampoo, ammonia, vinegar and if traces remain, dry cleaner.
Syrup	Apply shampoo and vinegar. If traces remain, apply dry cleaner.
Tar	Apply dry cleaner.
Urine	Apply vinegar and then shampoo, ammonia and more vinegar.
Vegetable oil	Apply dry cleaner. If traces remain, apply shampoo.
Vomit	Sponge with cool water. Apply shampoo, ammonia and vinegar.

Two Ways to Launder a Carpet by Machine

About once a year—or more often if they need it—you should clean your carpets with water and detergent. There are two kinds of machines you can use: foam-action shampooers like the one shown in the picture at right and the more thorough water-extraction cleaners like the one at the top of the opposite page. Both kinds can be rented, sometimes from grocery stores or drugstores.

Shampooers come with wheels, for shag carpets, and without, for low-pile carpets. In either form, a motorized rotary brush scrubs the carpet with a foam that comes from detergent and water mixed in a tank on the wand, usually in proportions of 1 to 12 (but check the container label). The foam loosens particles of dirt and dries around them; you then vacuum up both foam and dirt. Use only detergent intended for use on carpets; other household detergents, which are chemically different, require rinsing and may leave a sticky film that gathers soil, quickly making the carpet dirtier than it was before cleaning.

Shampooing is easier and less expensive than water extraction, but repeated shampooing leaves a build-up of detergent residue. Some professionals do not recommend shampooers at all; if you do use one, switch to a water-extraction machine at least every third cleaning, to remove detergent residue.

When renting a water-extraction cleaner, you will probably have to ask for a "steam" machine—the manufacturers use the word, in quotation marks, to imply high heat, although the machines actually dispense hot water. These cleaners spray a nonfoaming detergent solution onto the carpet under pressure and immediately suck up at least 75 per cent of the solution—and the dirt—from the carpet. To accomplish this, an extraction machine has two electric pumps as well as dispensing and receiving tanks. The machine is prepared by filling the dispensing tank to within 3 inches of the top with tap water (hot for synthetics, cold for wool). The detergent is added as directed on the container label—usually 2 ounces per gallon of water. Cover the bottom of the receiving tank with cold water plus 8 ounces of defoamer to neutralize sucked-up detergent residue.

Before starting, prepare the room by removing light furniture and protecting the rest with plastic sheeting under and around the legs. Vacuum the carpet and spot clean as described on page 123.

When either shampooing or cleaning by water extraction, be careful not to overwet the carpet and go easy on the solution-dispensing trigger. Excess water can cause the carpet's jute backing to shrink and pull the carpet from its fastenings. It can also dissolve the colors in the backing and pad, which then rise to the carpet surface and leave a stain.

For both methods, drying takes two or three hours—more on very humid days. You can speed drying, and restore pile depth, by brushing low-pile carpets with a clean broom and by sweeping shag carpets with a plastic shag rake. Put plastic sheeting under the legs of furniture as you move it back into the room, to prevent dampness from rusting the metal glides and staining the carpet.

Shampooing. With the brush rotating, push the shampooer over an area about 3 feet square while pressing the thumb trigger to release detergent solution. Then go over the area again without releasing detergent, scrubbing the foam into the carpet. Move on to the next area and repeat. Caution: do not dispense solution onto the same section of carpet twice, or you will overwet it. When the carpet dries, vacuum it and move the furniture back into the room.

Water-extraction cleaning. Turn on the machine's two pumps and, starting near a corner with the vacuum-head opening flat on the carpet, push the head away from you while squeezing the spray-release trigger. Move slowly; cover a swath 3 to 4 feet long in about 10 seconds. Stop spraying, and pull the vacuum head back over the sprayed area. Run the head over the area two or three times without spraying. Then clean another strip that overlaps the first. If a strip does not look clean, spray and vacuum again, but avoid overwetting; do not spray an area more than three times without letting it dry.

When the supply tank runs empty, turn off the switches, drain the receiving tank into a pail and wipe the tank clean of dirt and fibers before resuming the operation.

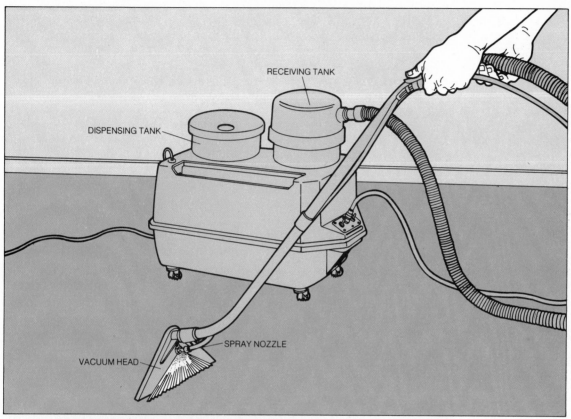

RECEIVING TANK

DISPENSING TANK

SPRAY NOZZLE

VACUUM HEAD

Cleaning stair carpet. If you are renting a water-extraction machine, you may also be able to rent hand tools for stair cleaning. Otherwise, make foam by squeezing a sponge repeatedly in carpet-shampoo solution, scoop up some of it with a clean scrub brush and work the foam into the carpet. Wring out the sponge in the shampoo solution and wipe up the excess foam. Brush or rake the pile erect. When the carpet has dried, go over it again with a stiff brush to loosen dried foam and dirt. Finally, vacuum.

Picture Credits

Sources for the illustrations in this book are shown below. Credits for pictures from left to right are separated by semicolons, from top to bottom by dashes. Cover—Fred Maroon. 6—Fred Maroon. 8 through 13—Drawings by Vicki Vebell. 14 through 23—Drawings by Fred Bigio from B-C Graphics. 24 through 27—Drawings by Walter Hilmers Jr. 28 through 35—Drawings by Peter McGinn. 36—Fred Maroon. 38 through 45—Drawings by Ray Skibinski. 47 through 49—Drawings by Fred Bigio from B-C Graphics. 50, 51—Drawings by Peter McGinn. 52 through 55—Drawings by Whitman Studio, Inc. 56 through 63—Drawings by John Massey. 64A—Richard Champion, Wilder Green, Architect, Mrs. Russell W. Davenport (associated with McMillin, Inc.), Interior Designer. 64B—Carla de Benedetti, Griffini and Montagni, Architects. 64C—Carla de Benedetti, Michele Sardirac, Architect—Charlie Wiesehahn, design by Melanie Zwerling for her apartment. 64D—Michael Dunne with Mary Gilliatt, Philippa Naess, Designer. 64E—Carla de Benedetti, Carla Venosta, Architect—Michael Dunne, Horace Gifford, Interior Designer. 64F—Leo Ferrante, Linda Garland, Interior Designer; Norman McGrath, Edward Knowles, Architect, Parish Hadley, Interior Designer, home of Robert Glenn Bernbaum. 64G—Gianni Berengo Gardin, Angelo Cortesi and Sergio Chiappa Catto, Architects. 64H—Fred Maroon. 66 through 75—Drawings by Vantage Art, Inc. 76 through 83—Drawings by Walter Hilmers Jr. 84 through 87—Drawings by Gerry Gallagher. 88 through 95—Drawings by Fred Bigio from B-C Graphics. 96—Fred Maroon. 98 through 109—Drawings by Great, Inc. 110, 111—Drawings by John Sagan. 112 through 115—Drawings by Ray Skibinski. 116 through 122—Drawings by Peter McGinn. 124, 125—Drawings by Dick Gage.

The following persons also assisted in the making of this volume by preparing the preliminary sketches from which the final illustrations were drawn: W. Hollis Anderson, Roger C. Essley, Fred Holz, Joan S. McGurren.

Acknowledgments

The index/glossary for this book was prepared by Mel Ingber. The editors also wish to thank the following: Alexandria Building Department, Alexandria, Va.; George Austin, Falls Church, Va.; Bruce W. Baiman, Brand Manager, Rinsenvac Products, Earl Grissmer Co., Inc., Indianapolis, Ind.; Bill Baker, American Plywood Association, Tacoma, Wash.; Eck Blankenship, Alexandria, Va.; Don Blevins, Ed Detwiler and Al Ozuna, Virginia Concrete, Springfield, Va.; Stanley Cohen, The Iron Shop, Broomal, Pa.; Howard Curtis, Heckmann Building Products, Chicago, Ill.; Harvey Dale, Covington, Va.; William Davis, Leslie-Locke Building Products Co., Lodi, Ohio; Fred Dillon and Wayne Dillon, Oxon Hill, Md.; R. K. Elliot, Marty's Floor Covering Co., Alexandria, Va.; Folk Flooring, Washington, D.C.; Beverly Ford, Antonio Troiano Tile & Marble Co., Inc., Beltsville, Md.; Eda Fountain, Earl Grissmer Co., Inc., Indianapolis, Ind.; Harry P. Harwood, Structural Engineer, Alexandria, Va.; Gene Hopkins and Bill Smith, Superior Carpet Shop, Inc., Washington, D.C.; William Jorgensen, Northern Virginia Flooring, Arlington, Va.; Jan Erik Knutsen, Naess & Co., New York, N.Y.; John Koehlein, Portland Cement Association, Arlington, Va.; Daniel Loewenthal, Bethesda, Md.; David Lynn Jr., Cherokee Wholesalers, Inc., Alexandria, Va.; Rudy Mendosa, James Steel Fabricators, Alexandria, Va.; Rosemary D. Merriam, Washington, D.C.; D. R. Norcross, Timber Engineering Co., Washington, D.C.; Joseph L. Owens, Assistant Manager, Northeastern Region, American Plywood Association, Annandale, Va.; Louis D. Romasco, Cherokee Wholesalers, Inc., Alexandria, Va.; Dale Schaffer, Del-Ray Rental Center, Alexandria, Va.; Andy Solinar, D & S Repair Service, Alexandria, Va.; Claude Taylor, Memphis Hardwood Flooring Co., Memphis, Tenn.; Robert E. Wood, Bethesda, Md.

The following persons also assisted in the writing of this book: Martin Fischhoff and Don Robertson.

Index/Glossary

Included in this index are definitions of many of the technical terms used in this book. Page references in italics indicate an illustration of the subject mentioned.

Adhesive-backed floors, 46
Adhesives: for cushion-back carpeting, 110; for hard floors, 32; for resilient floors, 28; for wood tiles, 46

Balusters: *vertical posts in balustrade.* Installing, *94-95;* replacing dovetailed, *70-71;* replacing doweled, *70;* replacing filleted, *71*
Balustrade: *railing on unenclosed edge of stairway.* Design of, 65; replacing balusters, *70-71;* structure, *67, 70*
Balustrade, installing, 88, 89, *90-95;* ordering parts, 89; tools for, 88
Basements: building stairway to, *76-79;* laying concrete floor in, 56, *57-61;* lowering floor, 56; resurfacing concrete floor, *62-63*
Blind-nailing: *nailing boards through edges so as to conceal nailheads.* Described, *12*
Blocking: *wood reinforcement for joists.* Installing, 8
Bridging: *bracing for joists.* Described, 14; installing, 8, 10; installing prefabricated steel, 16

Carpenter's clippers: *tool for cutting nails.* Described, 16
Carpeting: advantages of, 97; care, 123; construction types, 98; cushion-back, 98, 110, 122; examples, *64D-64E;* fiber types, 97; padding, *96,* 97; pile, 98; scraps, 116; tufted, *98*
Carpeting, cleaning: *124-125;* shampoo, 124; on stairs, *125;* water extraction, *125*
Carpeting, installing, 97, 98; cushion-back, *110-111;* cutting, *103-104;* laying, 103, *104-109;* padding, 98, 100, *102,* 112; pile direction, 98; planning layout, 98, *99;* seams, 97, 103, 110; on stairways, *112-115;* tackless strip, *100-101;* tools, 7, *96,* 97, 98, *106-107;* trimming, 109
Carpeting, repairing, 116; making tuft-setter, *116;* mending rips, *120-121;* patching, *118-119;* patching cushion-back, *122;* replacing pile, *116-117*
Carpeting, stain removal, 123
Carriages: *heavy notched boards supporting stair treads.* Described, *66;* dimensions, 84

Concrete: hand-mixing, 34; ready-mix, 56, 60
Concrete floors, 37; as base for tile, 62; checking for moisture, 38; cleaning and protecting, 35; patching, *34-35;* structure in basement, 56
Concrete floors, laying, 56; building forms, *58-59;* estimating quantity of concrete, 60; new surfaces, *62-63;* pouring concrete, 56, *60-61;* preparing basement floor, 56, *57;* over wood subfloor, 62

Floating floor: *floor of noise-reducing construction.* Building, 39
Flooring: hardwood, 40; mass production, 37; materials, 7, 37; synthetic, 37
Floors: in damp areas, 37; examples of, *64B-64E;* new prominence of, 64; opening for stairway, *76-79;* painted, 64, *64C;* strengthening for spiral stairway, 80; structure, *8, 10;* subfloor, *8;* underlayment, 8
Floors, hard: *floors of concrete, stone or ceramic.* Care of, 32; checking concrete for moisture, 38; sealing and painting concrete, 35; stain removal from concrete, 35. *See also* Concrete floors, laying; Stone floors, laying; Tile, ceramic; Tile, stone; Tile floors, laying ceramic
Floors, refinishing wood: equipment, 24, *25;* finishes, 26, *27;* sanding, 6, 7, *24-25;* sealing, 26; stain removal, 26
Floors, repairing hard, 32; painting concrete, 32; patching concrete, 32, *34-35;* replacing cracked tiles, *32-33;* resurfacing concrete, *62-63*
Floors, repairing resilient, *28-31;* blisters in linoleum, *31;* cementing tiles, *29;* filling holes, *28, 29;* patching sheet type, *30;* replacing sections, *28, 29*
Floors, repairing structure of, 7; girders, 14, 18; installing blocking, 8; installing bridging, 8, *10;* jacking, *15;* jacks for, 14, *15;* joists, 14, *16-17;* replacing girders, *20-23;* replacing posts, 14, *18-19;* sags, 14, *15-23*
Floors, repairing wood, 8-13; cracks, 8, *24;* replacing damaged boards, 8, *11-13;* squeaks, 8, *9-10*
Floors, resilient: *elastically compressible tile or sheet flooring.* Care of, 28, 31; materials and characteristics, 37, 46; stain removal, 31. *See also* Tile floors, laying resilient

Footings: *concrete supports for load-bearing posts.* Pouring concrete, 18, 19

Girders: *horizontal structural members supporting joists.* Repairing sags, *18-19,* 20; replacing, *20-23*
Gooseneck: *piece of balustrade connecting railing to upper newel.* Described, 67; installing, 89, *92-94*
Grout: *filler for spaces between tiles.* Applying to floor, 32, 33, *55*

Handrails, stairway, 67; building, 84; proportions and placement, 65
Hardwood flooring. *See* Floors, refinishing wood; Floors, repairing wood; Wood flooring

Joists: *horizontal supports for floors.* Doubling, 16; repairing sagging, 14, *15-17;* replacing, 16, *17*

Knee-kicker: *tool used to fasten carpet to tackless strip.* Described, 96, 97; use, *106-107, 108*

Linoleum: flattening bulges in, *31;* invention of, 37. *See also* Sheet flooring, laying

Miter box, renting, 6
Mortar: for flagstone, 55; for tile floors, 52

Nail claw: *tool for pulling nails.* Described, 16
Nailer, power, 7; described, *36, 37,* 40; use, 37, 40, 42
Newel posts: *structural vertical members of balustrade.* Described, 67; installing, 89, *90, 91-92;* tightening, *71*
Noise-reducing floor construction, *39*
Nosing: *rounded front edge of stair tread.* Described, 66, 67; dimensions, 84

Padding: *cushioning layer under carpeting.* Described, 96, 97, 100; installing, 100, *102;* installing on stairways, *113;* for stairways, 112
Paints for concrete, 32, 35
Parquet: *wood tile.* Described, 46, 49; laying, 46, *49. See also* Tile floors, laying wood
Pitch block: *guide used in installing stairway balustrade.* Described, 89; use, 92
Plywood, for flooring, 7

Risers: *vertical boards between stair treads.* Size, 84

Sandpaper, for floors, 24
Sealer, floor: *coating that seals wood pores and accents the grain.* Applying to wood, 24
Seaming tape, hot-melt: *material used to join pieces of carpet.* Described, 97; use, 103, *105*
Sheet flooring, laying, 46, 50; adhesives, 28, 50; described, 50; in large areas, 50; shaping sheets, *50-51*; in small areas, *50-51*. *See also* Floors, resilient
Square, framing: *right-angled ruler.* Use, 85
Stains, removing from floor: from carpeting, 123; from concrete, 35; from resilient materials, 31; from wood, 26
Stairways: carriage, 66; clearances, 76; disappearing, 80; examples, 64, *64A, 64F-64G;* materials, 7; prefabricated, 67; new prominence of, 64, 64F; rise and run, *84;* safety considerations, 65; steepness, 65, 84; structures, 66-67, 68, 84
Stairways, building simple, *84-87*
Stairways, carpeting, *112-115;* estimating materials, 112; padding, 112
Stairways, installing: disappearing, *80-81;* factory-built, *88-95;* opening floor, *76-79;* spiral, *80, 82-83;* tools, 7; writing specifications for, 88
Stairways, iron spiral: installing, 80, *82-83;* kits, *64H,* 65, 80; structure, *81*
Stairways, repairing wood, 66; balustrade, *70-71;* gluing and screwing, 66; loose newel post, *71;* replacing treads, *72-75;* squeaks in carriage-type, *68-69;* squeaks in prefabricated, 69
Stone floors, laying, 52; on concrete, *52-55;* flagstone, *55*
Stretcher, power: *carpet-laying tool.* Use, 106, *107,* 108
Stringers: *boards fit against ends of stair treads and risers.* Dimensions, *84;* housed, *67;* skirt, 66
Subfloor: *rough floor on which finished floor is laid.* Described, *8;* laying, 38

Tackless strip: *wood strip with embedded tacks for fastening carpeting.* Described, *96, 97, 100;* installing, *100-101;* installing on stairways, *113;* reusing, 98; types, 100
Tile, ceramic, 52; cutting, 33; types, 52. *See also* Floors, hard
Tile, stone, 52; types, 52
Tile floors, laying ceramic, 46, 52; on concrete, *52-55*
Tile floors, laying resilient, 46, *48;* adhesives for, 28, 46; over concrete, 46; dry run, *47;* estimating materials, 46; preparations for, 46, 47; over wood, 46. *See also* Floors, resilient
Tile floors, laying wood, 46, *49;* adhesives, 46; dry run, 47; estimating materials, 46; patterns, 49; preparations for, 46, *47,* 49
Treads, stairway: *horizontal surfaces of stairs.* Bullnose, *67;* installing bullnose, *90;* joints, *68;* landing, 89, *91;* materials, 84; nosing, 66, 67; repairing squeaky, *68-69;* replacing, *72-75;* size, 65, 84; surface, 65
Troweler, power: *gasoline-powered multibladed trowel.* Described, 7; use, 62, 63
Tuft setter: *carpet repair tool.* Making, *116;* use, *117*

Underlayment: *moistureproof and sound-deadening layer between subfloor and finished floor.* Damage and repair of, 28; described, *8*

Volute: *spiral end of railing.* Described, 67, *89*

Wood flooring: buying, 40; grades and sizes, 40; uses, 37. *See also* Floors, repairing wood
Wood floors, laying, *38-45;* boards, 40; over concrete, 38, *39;* preparation for, *38-41;* over tile, 38; wide planking, *45. See also* Tile floors, laying wood